Juvenile Impressions of Plant City — A Collection of Playful Stories

Jim Helms

Dedication

This collection of stories is dedicated to the loving memory of Betsy Stubbs (Bedgood).

Me with my first best friend

Preface

These 35 stories offer a playful telling of my observations
and feelings about growing up in and moving on from
Plant City, Florida. Subjects like love and rejection,
friendships made and lost, and descriptions of the strong-
willed women in my life are central to the telling.
Hopefully, the reader will enjoy the stories singly or as a
whole. Most of the stories have multiple vignettes, which
are not always consistent with the chronology of the
preceding or following story.

This work begins as fairly fictional and becomes less
embellished as it progresses. The stories are sorted into
seven parts based on my age. When the stories become
more fanciful, I use present tense and signal this with a
series of dots (...........................). The stories also generally
become longer and a bit more sophisticated as I grow up—
but hopefully, still playful in nature. Characters, names,
events, incidents, and locales are mostly either products of
my imagination or used in a fictitional way. In several
instances, the names of individuals and places, identifying
characteristics, and details have been changed.

The work includes places and activities that engaged me,
as well as how I tried to entertain myself and others. Many
of my blemishes are revealed, and occasionally a virtue.
Although some of the stories are largely make-believe, all
of them move in the general direction of truth. The stories
are more psychological than sociological.

Table of Contents

Adolescent

Teen

Groan-up

Acknowledgements

Part One – Tyke

Bethey, Gweenie, Johnnie

As a very small boy, I had a "lithp" and a "stuh-ssstuuuh-sstuudder," and I couldn't pronounce *R*s—my speech resembled a juicy mix of Daffy Duck, Porky Pig, and Elmer Fudd. I loved to talk and when I was understood it made up for my cartoon-like impediment. I sucked my right thumb such that it was half again as large as my left. I invariably wet the bed at night. My older sister, Judy, thought me disgusting and a waste of flesh. She would prefer that I just leave. I must have had something going for me though, because my Mama and Pop loved me very much. In another 15 years or so, Judy would too.

Bethey

"Bethey Thubbth" was my best friend before my memories began. She was supposed to be my future bride. Everyone said so. My parents and hers had been best friends since before we were born. The Stubbs family's first son was the same age as Judy, and I was a year younger than Betsy. Papa and Mama Thubbth had lived next to us when we lived on Warnell Street in eastern Plant City. After Pop bought the house on Ferrell Street using the GI Bill, Gil "Papa" Stubbs bought the new house next door.

Betsy was my first best friend. We were completely loyal to one another; we kept each other's secrets and never lied to each other. At Hiawatha Kindergarten and then elementary school, we saw increasingly less of each other because she was a year ahead of me. At home, though, we continued to play together, along with the other kids on the block. We played outdoor games like Red Light, Mother May I?, Hide and Seek, and Simon Says. We learned to ride our bikes together on Ferrell Street. We jumped rope. In the warmer months, we went to Robinson's swimming pool to splash for hours.

Me and Betsy at the Strawberry Festival Children's Parade

Betsy and I had a secret clubhouse in our back yard where we put puzzles together and played jacks, checkers, pick-up sticks, and card games like Go Fish, Old Maid, and Rummy. You could only enter with a password that changed weekly. When back in our homes, we watched *Howdy Doody*, *Romper Room*, and later, *Captain Kangaroo* and *The Mickey Mouse Club*. Our relationship was full of trust and fun.

We never dated, but my affection for her and her parents was lifelong. We seldom saw each other after my family moved, but she had shown me that girls make the finest best friends. Even though we didn't marry, I knew when I did, it would be to someone like Betsy: someone guileless, trusting, and kind.

Gweenie

Gweenie was one of my three earliest and closest friends when we lived on Ferrell Street. Our family had mostly feral cats around and under our home. They were fine outdoor specimens and sometimes affectionate, but I wanted a dog for my birthday. After some hesitation, Mama and Pop agreed we would become dog owners. Although I was too young to pick out the pup, I had permission to name the new member of our family.

When prompted by Pop to offer some suggestions, I was at a loss. Pop asked, "What color is the puppy?" I only knew one color. I replied, "Gween." Mama and Pop decided that was close enough. I suspect Judy objected, but, because of my speech deficiency, "Gweenie" was the pup's given name.

Gweenie and me with my light green frosted birthday cake

We got Gweenie a couple of days before my birthday. I told my parents I wanted a gween birthday to go with my gween dog. Mama baked a cake with a chocolate center dyed a deep green and pale green mint frosting. I also got dark green pajamas that made me look like a tiny version of one of Robin Hood's Merrie Men. It was a glorious birthday.

Gweenie was "my" dog. We were such good pals. He made me giggle, laugh, and shriek with joy. He didn't bite, but he did keep running away—often for a day or two at a time. We had no leash laws in Plant City, and our family didn't have a fenced yard.

One summer afternoon, while playing on our porch, and a few months after getting Gweenie, a horse—which I thought were "big qween dogs"—ran across our front yard. Gweenie began chasing it. I was amazed and delighted. It may have been the first time I saw a horse in real life; the horses in cowboy movies weren't real at all to me, although I believed in their riders.

Gweenie could not be found that afternoon. We looked; we sent out scouts; we waited. We asked the neighbors, who were much more interested in the mystery horse than the missing pup. We never found Gweenie, and no one knew where the horse came from or where it ended up.

I grieved and wept, but later that week, one of the she-cats under our house had kittens. Although I missed Gweenie greatly, the kittens distracted me. I believed Gweenie had run off with the horse and I believed they were living together happily. I imagined them to be jolly friends much like Roy Rogers' horse, Trigger, and his dog, Bullet.

Although he had abandoned me, I hoped the best for him. After a few months, the memory of Gweenie faded, but it never left completely.

Johnnie

At a young age, I had a friend named Johnnie, who lived three doors down from us. He was probably 14 or 15, but he was no more than four feet tall. He had an oversized head. We shared the same vocabulary range and mental capabilities.

Our neighborhood was on the edge of town, and behind our houses was farmland. Johnnie's family had been there long before we moved into our new VA cracker box tract home. Johnnie's family had a few acres of vegetables and they kept chickens; they were country.

At our house, we saw grey squirrels, armadillos, an occasional rabbit, and pocket gophers. (We never saw an actual gopher, but our yard always had a half-dozen or so mounds we called salamander hills that were dug by pocket gophers.) Oh, and we had lots of ant hills in our yard, but I didn't consider ants to be animals then. We had no chickens.

Pop did not approve of my friend or his family. He got upset when he learned that I had been to Johnnie's. He said he wanted me to play with kids my own age. Pop said Johnnie had water on the brain when he was born; I would learn much later this was hydrocephalus, which can reduce one's mental and physical abilities.

But Johnnie and his family were fun. He seldom left his yard, and we were always supervised by his mom or other adults in the family.

I loved going to Johnnie's house. His mom once showed us how to catch, kill, and dress a chicken. It was a fascinating show of running, swooping, snatching, squawking, beheading, wing-flapping, blood, guts, and feathers.

We'd climb all over his dad's tractor, sit in the seat, and play farmer. I remember Hank Williams and Kitty Wells singing on the radio. It was always tuned to a country station, which was not the kind of music played at our house.

Pop told me that Johnnie was not only too old for me, but he was mentally disabled. I didn't know what that meant. Pop insisted I stop visiting him, and I obeyed. I still had lots of friends my age on our block, but I missed Johnnie, his family, and his radio. Pop's admonition to stay away from Johnnie and his mental health issues made me aware for the first time of mental illness. I regret abandoning my friendship with Johnnie. He deserved better.

Pop and me

Maid

Mary

Fah had one eye. I think I swallowed the other. Mary replaced the missing eye with a clear, large button. Fah looked like Mr. Peanut with his monocle eyepiece and peanut color. Unlike Mr. Peanut, his head drooped from side to side. He was the wisest of my three bears, and the oldest. He had been there when my mother told me about Pooh, that "silly bear."

My other two teddy bears had furry coats—one chocolate brown, the other pale brown. They smelled like mohair. Fah had almost no coat left. He'd had a couple of modestly successful surgeries to replace some of his innards. He smelled like me. I loved Fah, as did Mary.

Pop and Mama wanted to replace Fah. I objected. He must have looked quite sad to others, though. When I told Mary, she not only sympathized with me, she intervened, as best her position allowed. Whatever she said, it worked. I kept Fah until I lost interest in him.

Mary (c. 1950)

All of my memories of Mary are joyful. She babysat me and was my playmate and caregiver for a couple of years, beginning around age three. We loved each other and were loyal and caring friends.

She made me fun food. I made her laugh. We played games no one else in my family ever knew about—cool games with utensils from the kitchen, Pop's ashtrays, and small trinkets she'd bring with her. She showed me how to make an army, or a posse, or a navy of boats with old bottle caps. When the bad soldiers got killed or the outlaws got shot or the ships sank, we turned the shiny tops of the bottle caps upside down so the "dead" cork was showing.

Mary kept me safe, dry, and happy. Did I mention she saved Fah?

Maids were abundant in Plant City and in my family's households. They were part of my life from age three until my late teens. Not every white family had a maid; having one was a measure of making it to the middle class. These African American women were housekeepers, laundresses, cooks, nannies, and sometimes companions.

Most maids worked for cash and very little of it. They often had families of their own, and certainly domestic duties waited for them at their homes when they finished working at ours. It wasn't unusual for their employers to fail to have Social Security deductions taken out of their pay to protect them in old age.

Of course, they all lived in "Colored Town." That other Plant City "town" was located across the railroad tracks that ran along U.S. Highway 92. It looked run-down. We rode our bicycles everywhere in Plant City, but never there.

Our family was on the lower edge of lower middle class. I suspect my grandparents Foster or Helms helped pay Mary's wages. My mother, a schoolteacher, had to work. She provided most of our income, since Pop was a struggling car salesman. She worked outside the home during the day, as did all the women in our extended family, so Mary's help was essential.

I was too soon registered for kindergarten with Mrs. W. M. (Mary Ellen) Henry. I wasn't sure what that would be like, but Mary assured me I would love it. She told me that I would get real smart and make all kinds of new friends. But I loved my life at home. I was sure I was smart enough—way smarter than my bears. I had my friends Betsy next door, the twins two doors down, and Malcolm and Ronnie across the street.

Fall came, and the Hiawatha tribe set up camp in Mrs. Henry's enclosed garage. She was very nice. All 23 of us had our own little desks and chairs. Mrs. Henry had a neat working cuckoo clock on her kitchen wall that fascinated all of us Hiawathans. The back yard had room to run and run and an inner tube tire swing tied to the limb of a massive oak tree. Hiawatha was preparing me for Wilson Elementary School the next year. It provided me with a set of peers whom I loved and formed cherished friendships with.

Mrs. Henry wrote to my parents in November 1952, "Jim is completely relaxed. He's been really running with the gang for the last few weeks. He seems to get along nicely on the playground. We have very few complaints about his not sharing, etc." She concluded, "I'm so pleased that he seems so happy at kindergarten." Her report included a handwritten notation that served as an invoice. The cost to be a member of the Tribe of Hiawatha was $8 per week.

I came home one day, and Mary was gone. I never saw her again. But Mary was right: I loved kindergarten. I was learning all kinds of interesting stuff—like finger-painting—and I began to grasp numbers and letters. I was making lots of new friends.

Still, I never got to hug Mary goodbye, and she never got to hug me goodbye. I was distraught. I cried; I sobbed; I wailed for Mary. I threw a couple of hardy tantrums. Nothing worked; no Mary.

Pop would later explain that he found drops of her dipping snuff on the sheets on my parents' bed. He said that was filthy. Pop was a heavy smoker, and there were ashtrays all over the house full of cigarette butts. His explanation never satisfied me. That made me miss her more.

My graduation from kindergarten

Lillian

Lillian was my grandmother Zula's maid. She was a great cook. Zula would say that she had taught Lillian about southern cooking. Maybe. Whoever taught her, she mastered it and prepared amazing meals; I've never tasted better.

Our whole family dined there regularly. On weekdays, lunch at Zula's required two seatings. Lillian prepared two meat courses, at least three fresh vegetables, a huge jug of sweetened iced tea, a dessert, and a dozen hoecakes, known to us as "cornbread" and to others, "Johnnycakes."

While the Helms family ate—one shift from noon to 1, the other from 1 to 2—Lillian would be at the stove cooking fresh hot cornbread for the 12 or so diners.

When it was time for more fresh cornbread to be brought to the table, rather than yell at Lillian in the kitchen, we'd ring a small red bell on the table to get her attention. When more tea was needed, a simple shake of the ice in the bottom of the glass would bring Lillian with another pitcher.

Lillian's and Zula's dinner bell

Zula and her husband, Lem, owned a women's dress shop in downtown Plant City. It was the first retail store in town exclusively selling women's dresses. Helms Dress Shop was one of the first clothing stores in Plant City to trade with blacks.

Zula would drive the six blocks home from the store and join the noon crowd, while Lem would take his lunch at one, following her return to the store. They had a fine formal dining room, but lunch was served in a breakfast nook off of the kitchen that overlooked the back yard. The table in the nook was large, with pew-like benches on each side against the walls; two walls were all casement windows. You had to slide your way into your place at the table.

I began eating at Zula's during summer breaks in elementary school, a tradition that continued through junior high and high school. During seventh grade at Tomlin, I had a health issue that led to nasty-looking sores on my legs. Although it was never diagnosed, Dr. Clarke Weeks, whose office was over White's Central Pharmacy, recommended that I eat more nutritiously. I got a daily medical pass to go to Zula's for lunch. My legs healed in a few months, thanks in no small part to Lillian's cooking.

I also went into the "Lillian's cornbread" retail sales business. After lunch, during my entire attendance at Tomlin, I wrapped two or three of those tasty jewels in tin foil, brought them back the five blocks to school, and sold them to my classmates for a nickel.

It was a racket, because I never shared my profits with Lillian. That's regrettable; she probably would have found better use for the money. I spent my 100% profits on candy like Zero bars, Atomic Fireballs, Tops bubble gum, and Sugar Daddies, none of which Dr. Weeks had in mind when he prescribed a healthier diet.

Lillian was vital to the well-being and happiness of my extended family. The smells, texture, flavor, and nutritional benefits of her cuisine have stayed with me.

Lorraine

Lorraine was in her thirties when she began working for my parents. By then, childcare responsibilities had ebbed in our house. A part-time housekeeper, she did all the laundry and ironing for our family. Lorraine didn't cook for us, however.

Lorraine was our maid until I went to college, but while still working for us, she accepted a job at NuWay Cleaners, where she operated the dry cleaning machines. Soon she was promoted to a customer-facing job. She was one of the first maids I knew to make the transition from domestic service to customer service.

Although many maids were accepted members of the family employing them and were often loved and respected—particularly by the children they tended—it wasn't sustainable employment. None were full members of the wider white community where they lived in the Deep South. Progress in that arena would come later as the maid/nanny industry fractured.

Hole

Disporched

The porch was eaten at dawn. Mr. Mullins had just put a pot of coffee on and was walking to the front door to get the morning paper. Then the world ruptured. The entire house shook, and Mr. Mullins was thrown to the floor. The sound was like a grove of trees being knocked down with a shattering crack and splintering of timber.

Mr. Mullins ran to the bedroom and saw his wife sitting upright in bed. She was pale and silent, and there were tears on her cheeks. He immediately said, "Let me help you." They went to work with practiced fingers and put her prosthetic leg on. Their son, Mike, was standing in the doorway, asking repeatedly, "What's happening? What's happening? What's happening?"

It was my summer between Hiawatha Kindergarten and first grade at Wilson Elementary. When the earth started eating the Mullins' porch next door, I was sleeping, but the noise got my full attention. I had no idea what was going on in the half-light, but I was pretty sure I was getting scared.

My sister, Judy, looked over with a face of angry terror; her eyes suggested whatever was happening was my fault. Pop ran by our bedroom door. Right behind him, Mama rushed into the room. "Get up, hold my hand, come with me," all came rushing out in one breathless shout. The three of us ran to the back door, where Pop was yelling for us to follow him.

Making our way down the back steps in the early light, we saw a hole in the ground where the Mullins' porch should have been. It was the largest hole I'd ever seen. Now I *was* scared.

I would have peed myself, except I had done so earlier in the night when I was quite comfortable in my own bed; I have no doubt some of our neighbors were not as resourceful. The Mullins family was standing in their back yard, where we joined them.

No one spoke at first. Then, a series of "Are you all right?" and "What happened?" Other neighbors joined us, and Pop went back inside to call the police.

The Mullins Hole was estimated to be about 20 feet deep. At the bottom were scattered remains of the porch. A green steel rocking chair was sticking out of the ooze at the bottom of the pit. Even after the police showed up, no one approached the lip of the sinkhole for fear it would expand and collapse.

I began to cry and tremble. My mother held me in her arms, and Mrs. Mullins stroked my head. I quieted when the fire engine arrived. As the men in their gear climbed off the trucks, my fear was replaced with wonder.

Later, Pop would explain that the geology of Florida causes sinkholes. Beneath the green and sandy surface of West/Central Florida is porous limestone, which can hold immense tracts of water in underground aquifers. Sinkholes form when the surface layer of earth above those aquifers caves in. Florida sinkholes vary in depth from 3 to over 1000 feet. Ferrell Street got off light.

Fear, however, became deep-seated in our neighborhood, and the closer you lived to the Mullins Hole, the more piercing the anxiety. Our porch was within 15 feet of the side of the sinkhole. Our lives were affected by the Mullins Hole. Everything would change.

Cards and Coffee

I was loving life on Ferrell Street. Mrs. Mullins, who lost her right leg just above the knee in an auto accident years before, taught me how to drink coffee. She'd get us both cups and fill mine three-fourths with whole milk, adding just enough coffee to give my drink a custard color and two heaping teaspoons of sugar. I loved my coffee with her. Over a few weeks' span, I moved on to one-fourth milk/three-fourths coffee, with one teaspoon of sugar.

We'd drink our coffee at her dining table while she patiently taught me solitaire. By then, I knew my numbers pretty well and the face cards were easy enough to learn. Every few hands, when the cards had been played into four neat piles of ace through king, in suit, Mrs. Mullins and I would celebrate with cheers and a second cup of coffee.

Mrs. Mullins and our other next-door neighbor, Mama Stubbs, were my loving friends and substitute babysitters for Mary, our maid. The Mullins never spent another night in the house with the hole. They still visited, but they were largely out of our lives.

Foster Care

That morning, all the grownups in the family discussed what we should do. Pop and Mama decided that staying with my paternal grandparents Helms was impractical, since their youngest son, Bobby, who was in high school, lived with them. Instead, Mama, Judy, and I would move in temporarily with my maternal grandparents, "Pampa" Roy Foster and "Mom" Zola Foster, in south Plant City.

We started moving our clothes and some of our belongings to the Fosters' the afternoon of the sinkhole. Pop helped with the move, but he stayed at the Ferrell Street house that night and for weeks to come.

We came back to Ferrell Street regularly to visit our friends. Judy and I weren't allowed to go into our house, but we watched from across the street, as dump truck after dump truck filled the Mullins Hole with rocks and dirt. That work was as interesting as anything I'd seen. It was loud, dusty labor—men bustling and engaged in a dozen different noisy jobs—all centered on filling the hole. The whole Mullins house was bulldozed soon after.

I loved all of my family, and staying with Mom and Pampa Foster would be fun. Pampa had a bull in the pasture behind his house, and I was allowed to name him "Bullie." Pampa trained him to walk up to the fence, stick his massive two-horned head under the top board, and poke it through so Pampa could pat it.

Pampa also trained Bullie to butt me if I tried to pat his head as Pampa did. Bullie would raise his head against my chest, push, and dump me solidly on my bottom. I was never hurt (I bounced well at that age), but I never wised up either. That little schtick was played over and over to the delight of both Pampa and me.

Pampa was a retired mail carrier, and he and Mom Foster and their only child, Keeta—my mother—had weathered the Great Depression well. He was an amateur carpenter who kept adding rooms to their seven-room house, so there was plenty of room for three more houseguests. His hammer and saw skills were decent.

His electrical skills were not. Several rooms had light switches that controlled nothing, and he had a strong preference for 20-watt bulbs. He installed several sconces with candelabra bulbs—none of which worked. He compensated for the cave-like aspect of his home by installing as many windows as possible. During the day, it was very bright inside and at night, most night-like.

Pampa and Mom were from Sedan, in southeast Kansas, close to the Oklahoma border. Think flint hills, mesa country with cattle, and a sprinkling of oil wells, instead of flat wheat fields. Roy taught school as a young man, and Zola was one of his students.

After moving around Kansas and Oklahoma, they moved to Texas and then New Mexico with the U.S. Post Office. Zola got her teaching certificate—typing and shorthand were her specialties. They moved to Plant City in the late 1930s, where she taught high school and he started a successful real estate career after retiring from the Post Office.

My grandparents, Roy and Zola Foster, 1927

Pampa and Mom Foster had a television, a splendid luxury for Judy and me. When it was just the two of us camped out in front of the TV, Judy chose what we watched, of course, she being always in charge. I liked all the shows Judy selected, but I adored Roy Rogers as the "King of Cowboys"; he and Trigger occupied a preeminent place in my heart.

We went to my other grandmother Zula's house for lunch occasionally, but our big meal was supper at the Fosters'. The cornbread changed dramatically between Zula's and Zola's and not for the better. Zola's was cooked in the oven, for no good reason. With a little drizzle of maple syrup, it became much tastier, but it was closer to dessert than the meal-making cornbread that Zula's cook, Lillian, made.

Pop visited us every day when he got off work. He visited us after dinner, but he never stayed long. I missed him at night and in the mornings. Pampa and Mom Foster did not speak to Pop, nor he to them, and there were never any hugs.

Lyin'

Carvin'

A fork would work perfectly. Since I'd sliced halfway
through my left index finger a few months earlier, I had lost
all interest in knives. The piano bench was of a dark brown
wood and heavily polished. My sister, Judy, owned the
piano. She made sure everyone understood that it was "her
piano."

I had been caught climbing from the bench to the upright's
keyboard and onto the top of the piano to get to some
bananas that my mother had placed there (to keep away
from me). Reportedly, I got a big laugh from Mama when
she caught me eating one of the out-of-reach bananas, with
my small legs dangling over the edge of the piano. She
started calling me "gabby monkey boy." I was lightly
scolded for my monkey act and told repeatedly not to touch
the piano. Nothing was said about the bench.

Judy had told on me twice that week already. She had
taken great pride and delight in telling Pop and Mama that
I sneaked into the kitchen and ate half of a pineapple
upside-down cake. The next day, she'd tattled on me
about playing with matches. I found a dinner fork in the
kitchen easy enough and began my revenge.

I would try my best to carve "Judy" into the top of the
bench. I figured everyone would think Judy had done it
herself and I would have my justice. I held the fork in my
little hand the way I'd seen grownups hold pencils. Placing
the sharp point of a prong on the top of the bench, I

pressed down. Nothing appeared. I pressed harder, sliding my hand down the fork.

I began "Judy" with the curve in the J. My hand slipped; I could see a scratch, but it was crooked. I decided it was an acceptable start and started on the straight line that would top off my J. My hand was pretty unstable, and it was not a very clean job. The J looked more like a checkmark than a letter. The u-d-y was little better. I suspected my work ... well, wouldn't. I began to practice my denial.

I was a prolific, stubborn, lousy liar. I told lies not only to hide my relatively few imperfections and rare misdemeanors, but also because I just enjoyed "make believe." Cartoons were make believe, as were cowboy movies and comic books. Lying was my performance of make believe.

I refused to admit it when my make believe unraveled in the face of truth and reality. Why end the fun? Mama almost always believed my lies, but my refusal to admit a falsehood infuriated Pop. When he confronted me with the consequences of defacing the bench, he told me if I didn't lie about it, he wouldn't switch me.

I had practiced my denial earnestly and wasn't going to waste that effort. I lied. I lied again. After the third or fourth swing of the switch from our yard (that I had to pick and bring to him myself), I caved. I admitted to the crime, and the switching stopped. The only thing I learned from that "lesson" was that Judy enjoyed it excessively.

Me and Judy, 1950 (notice how we naturally lean away from each other)

Sweet Loot

I was rummaging through the hall closet where several of my mother's older purses were kept. One of them felt heavier than the others. I opened the purse and found ten or so silver dollars, some dating back to the early 1900s. I took two of them (who would miss two?) and pocketed them cleanly. The next day, I rode my bike six blocks to the small store at Wheeler and English Streets, where they sold a great selection of candy.

Being quite clever, I only used one of the silver dollars. I even got change. I ate a whole row of Neccos on my leisurely ride home and hid the bag of remaining treats under my bed. As I went outside and started to cross the street, I saw Pop's car approach. He was home early. He stopped and called me over. All he said was, "Go inside." I had no clue why he would say that, having already forgotten where my financial independence came from.

He told me he had received a call from the candy store owner who told him I had purchased a large stock of candy earlier that day. "Where did you get the money, Jim?" he asked. "Oh, I've saved it up from the tooth fairy and Christmas," I replied with all the conviction a young boy could muster. Pop reached in his pocket and pulled out a silver dollar.

"What is that?" I asked almost convincingly. "This is what you stole, Jim," he declared. I denied it. I kept up my disavowal until the fourth or fifth swat. Pop never spanked hard; he rarely punished me. He felt this time he had to. I could tell he was disgusted having to do it. That may have upset me more than the passing pain to my bottom. I gave him back the other silver coin I'd taken, and he confiscated the candy. That last part hurt worse than the spanking.

BB

One year, the Fosters gave me a Red Ryder BB gun with the understanding that I would keep and shoot it only at their house, which was in a more rural setting on the south side of Plant City. I could hit a large tree from six feet about 20 percent of the time. I could miss squirrels at any range. I missed birds, leaves, tin cans, bottles, laundry hanging on the line, the shed by the pasture, the sun, Bullie the bull, and once, Judy. None of my prey had any idea they were in my sight, for the BB air gun made practically no noise and its range was limited to about ten yards. I did bag a receptionist once, though.

Across our grandparent Fosters' side yard sat the WPLA-AM radio station. The receptionist was seated with her back to the window facing the side yard. The window was open. I began my target practice by aiming at the antenna tower. I heard no ricochet, so I knew my shot was off. I tried again—same result, so I gave up on the tower. I decided the bushes below the tower were the thing. I shot at them, but I could see no movement in the leaves: a clear miss. It was getting boring, so I stopped shooting. I did not know my last errant BB hit her. I couldn't even see her. I didn't hear her shriek.

WPLA radio station

Going back inside, I heard the phone ring, and Mom Foster answered it. She announced after hanging up, "It was the radio station. Jim shot someone." I thought that impossible. Pampa gave me a spanking before I could deny it or formulate a lie. Pampa Foster wasn't really concerned about lies; he was much more focused on the crime. It was the only spanking I would ever get from him. He hit harder with his open hand than Pop, and it didn't seem to bother him at all.

I then got a very stern lecture from both of the Fosters. I was to apologize to the receptionist. I didn't fight back. Mom Foster took me to the station. When we met my unintended target, I said, "If I shot you, I'm sorry." Mom Foster would have none of that. She swatted my bottom, and I began apologizing heartily. The receptionist was not hurt, but she did have a tiny red spot at the base of her neck. I apologized some more. I was truly sorry for the pain I'd caused the receptionist. She seemed very nice. I was kind of glad I hadn't lied. I never shot the BB gun again.

Burnin'

The sofa was a total loss, but at that, not much of one. It was threadbare and well used by my family. It always had a bit of a stink to it, but the charcoal version of it was rank.

Judy and Mama had gone next door to the Stubbs'. I have always sneaked. It complements lyin'. I'm better at sneakin' than lyin'. One of my favorite sneaks was to crawl behind the sofa and hide. This particular day, I found a book of matches from the Columbia Restaurant in Tampa's Ybor City next to Pop's ashtray on the little table next to the couch. I brought the matches with me.

After lighting just a few of the matches, I lit one too close to the afghan that draped over the back of the couch. The flame leapt from the match to the afghan and crawled to the back of the couch. It was suddenly very scary in our living room. Smoke was starting to climb the wall behind and over me. I dropped the match book and ran to the front door. As I opened it, the smoke followed me.

Standing on the front porch, I started screaming.

Neighbors, including Mr. Stubbs and Mr. Clayton, and Judy and Mama ran to our smoking house. The men went inside and quickly dragged the sofa outside. Mrs. Stubbs turned on the garden hose and sprayed it. The few flames subsided quickly, but the smoke continued for an hour.

I knew I was in deep trouble. I wasn't hurt. I was getting lots of hugs. No damage was done to the house or the other furniture, but I had quite destroyed the sofa and afghan. There was so much going on in our house and yard, it took a while for questions about how the fire started, until Pop got home.

Pop saved me the trouble of coming up with a lie. He told me he wasn't going to spank or switch me. He said he had something else in mind for my punishment. I imagined being banished to my room, although that had never happened. Perhaps I'd be denied access to the radio, which also hadn't happened before. I kept guessing what lay in store most of the night. I became exhausted and finally went to sleep.

Next morning after breakfast, Pop was missing. I went outside to look at the sofa. Yep, it was done for. As I inspected the drenched, foul-smelling, charred remains, Pop drove up. He got out of his car with a cardboard box and told me to follow him.

We sort of marched to the back porch, and he told me to sit down on the steps. As I did, he placed the cardboard box within my reach. I looked inside and there were more matches inside than I'd ever seen—thousands of matches: wood matches in small boxes; matchbooks from all kinds of product promotions, retail stores, restaurants, and Florida attractions; and box after box of kitchen matches. It was fascinating.

Pop said I was to strike each match individually, blow it out, and put the expended match in a pile at my feet on the concrete step. I froze. I didn't think I was being rewarded for almost setting the house on fire, but this didn't feel like punishment, either. He told me to begin. I started with matchbooks. They were the most interesting, with images of all sorts in various colors and styles on their thin cardboard covers.

I enjoyed the first hour. Pop came out then and inspected my pile of burnt matches. He told me to take a break. After a pee and some water, I returned to my task. After about 90 minutes, I burned my finger. Although it hurt, it wasn't a serious burn and didn't blister.

I was given another break. It had stopped being fun. When I returned to it, I immediately burned another finger. That started a pattern of every few minutes getting another burn. I was in some pain but kept at it.

Pop came out and asked to see my hand. He determined I was fit enough to continue. I struck matches for close to four hours. I didn't make it through the entire box, but I had made a good dent in it. Pop and Mama tended to my slightly singed but not seriously damaged fingers with Bactine.

No more was said about the sofa—well, except for Judy, who beat the story to death over the next few years. She talked about it with a self-satisfied smirk, even as she said, "Thankfully, James wasn't killed and the house didn't burn down."

Burney

Rejection

"No. Keeta, It's either him or me." That was the answer my grandfather, Roy Foster, gave my mother when my Pop, L.K., asked Roy for my mother's hand in marriage in 1939. My grandmother, Zola, was standing next to Roy, and she didn't disagree. The Fosters believed my father couldn't properly support their daughter and probably wasn't good enough for her.

My mother and father, who were both 21 when L.K. proposed, did marry, despite the opposition of her parents. The young couple was determined, but the Fosters insisted that Keeta (Mama) get her college degree before they consented to the marriage.

Keeta returned to Oklahoma State College for Women for her last year of college and got her degree. Roy and Zola sent out invitations and attended the wedding, even though they thought the marriage was probably a mistake.

Keeta and L.K. while engaged

That was the backdrop when we had to move in with the Fosters after the sinkhole ate our neighbor's porch.

Although they lived within two miles of each other and resided in a town of a few thousand people, L.K. and Roy had barely spoken since my parent's wedding in 1941.

The soreness first appeared a couple of weeks after Mama, Judy, and I moved in with Pampa and Mom Foster, and it was getting worse. During our several weeks' stay, Pop continued to live in our house on Ferrell Street. When he visited us at night, he and the Fosters avoided each other.

They never spoke negatively about each other in front of me or Judy. The absence of affection between the Fosters and my father, however, was such an anomaly in our extended family in Plant City, it was jangling. It was like listening to an accomplished orchestra with the percussion section playing at a different tempo.

The silent but constant tension and conflict between Mama's parents and husband seemed to settle in her neck. The pain was on the left side at the base of her neck, just above her shoulder. It increased in intensity over the next several days, and it hurt constantly.

She went to local doctors, who conducted a series of medical tests. The doctors considered the pain to be neurological and suggested rest and aspirin. She was spending a large portion of the day in bed, even though she found it difficult to sleep. She wasn't sure she could teach again when school started in a few weeks.

Treating the pain with aspirin, she began exceeding the recommended dosage, so codeine was prescribed. At dinner one evening, she said, "I can't breathe." Her face was swollen, particularly her lips. She pleaded, "I'm suffocating." She said she had to go outside to get more air. Pampa helped her up from the table and led her to the garage. He assisted her into his open-air Jeep, raised the garage door, and sped off, heading down State Road 39 and Highway 60.

Later, we got a telephone call from Pampa, saying he and my mother were at the hospital. She'd had a reaction to the codeine. Pop arrived at the Fosters' and, when told the news, went to the hospital. Judy and I were frightened. We held each other for a few seconds, which was a great rarity and felt most awkward. We comforted each other nonetheless.

Railroad

A few days later, we moved to a rental house next to the railroad tracks. It was on Drane Street—where Franklin Street crossed the tracks. Pop and Mama had decided that they needed to live together under their own roof. I heard some of those discussions after her return from the emergency room. I could feel the tension through the closed door.

We were all relieved when Pop reunited with the rest of our family. The sinkhole had been filled and appeared to have stabilized, but not enough time had elapsed for the family to move back to our Ferrell Street home. Mama's neck pain began to subside, but she had a constant kink in her neck, and soreness developed that limited its motion. She had to turn her upper body to look to the right.

We didn't have a TV, nor did anyone else in our new neighborhood. We went back to listening to the radio. Shows such as *Amos and Andy*, *The Shadow*, and *The Lone Ranger* were featured weekly at our new house. I felt *Big John and Sparky* was the best radio show. Sparky was an elf who wanted to be a real boy. I was rooting for him. The 15-minute daily show started with, "Hi! Hey! Hello there!" "The Teddy Bears' Picnic" followed the greeting and became my favorite song; I sang it for anyone who listened, although I didn't need an audience.

....

A faraway, drawn-out whistle glides into my dream. A pause. Then four seconds later, two short whistles. Another pause. Another long blast. The bells begin, barely audible. I roll over. The metallic bells clang in one-second intervals. A long whistle, this time closer, followed by two short, one long whistle is the constant refrain. The train is approaching the city limits. A new set of bells jangle, closer. The two sets of crossing bells create a round-like chorus. The refrain repeats, and the verse ends.

I'm now awake and can faintly hear the diesel-electric engine. More ringing signals start. The whistles are now regular; each time the train approaches a public grade crossing, the four-note refrain is repeated. Another set of crossing bells begins as the train approaches the "diamond" crossover of the Atlantic Coast Railroad tracks (east/west line) and the Seaboard Air Line (north/south line) in downtown Plant City. It's the only place in the country where that intersection occurs.

Plant City's diamond crossover

It is a pleasing, harmonically repeated progression of bells, some distant, some close. As the train approaches the Franklin Street crossing by our house, the whistle repeats its song. The track's rumble provides percussion as the train passes by my bedroom window. The house trembles slightly in sync with the train. As the train passes, a change in pitch occurs that I'd later understand as the Doppler affect. At my young age, I just know it is haunting, yet peaceful. It gently puts me back to sleep.

....

Flux

We were living four blocks from our grandparents Helms, where we usually ate our weekday lunches with our grandmother Zula. It was wonderful to have her fried hoecakes regularly again. Judy and I were taken to our old neighborhood on weekends to play with our friends. I was registered for school at Burney Elementary based on the address of our new residence. The new school was close to the Fosters' house, which Judy and I often visited and where we caught up on our TV shows.

I had never considered going anywhere but Wilson Elementary, two blocks from our Ferrell Street home.

That's where all my friends went. None of my fellow graduates from Mary Ellen's Hiawatha Kindergarten went to Burney. Judy also wanted to return to Wilson, having attended there until the sinkhole changed everything.

My only memories of Burney are sitting in my mother's car in front of the school waiting for Judy's class to be dismissed an hour after my class was dismissed. Mama brought comic books with her, and we passed the time reading them together. I learned to read in a car rather than at school. Mama would read me a comic book, like *Casper the Friendly Ghost*, and then hand it to me so I could try to read it, with her prompting me. I got pretty good after a couple of months. I made no friends at Burney.

Mama's neck was now permanently stiff, and she had limited mobility. The piercing pain had been replaced with a tight-feeling golf ball-sized knot that was always sore. The only sharp pain she felt was when she tried to look to the right. Judy and Pop took turns massaging it, and she started going to a chiropractor. Her neck soreness continued for years. She eventually improved, thanks to new antidepressant drugs, but the stiffness in her neck was permanent.

The transfer back to Wilson was planned for after the holidays. I thought the close-up trains were exciting and fun on Drane Street, but I knew with the windows open at our home on Ferrell Street, I could hear the trains and signals at night and the house wouldn't shake.

Part Two – Kid

Wilson

Infirm

"He missed about three weeks of school with measles (and what the doctor thought might have been polio) in January just before we transferred him," my mother wrote to Miss Grace Platt, my first grade teacher, on April 8, 1954.

In that year, a parent's worst fear was polio (poliomyelitis). The infectious disease caused by a virus resulted in 35,000 cases reported in 1953, with 1,450 deaths in the United States. Polio was particularly devastating to very young children. Infected children often showed no symptoms of polio, making it difficult to diagnose. One in 200 infections led to irreversible paralysis. Among those paralyzed, 5 to 10 percent died when their breathing muscles became immobilized: death at its most brutal.

I didn't have polio; the measles were bad enough. In the 1950s, nearly all children got measles by the time they were 15. An effective vaccine would be developed in the early 1960s. I shook the rubella virus after three weeks.

My family had been living on Drane Street following our temporary relocation caused by the sinkhole next door to our home on Ferrell Street. I attended school in south Plant City during the first six months of the school year. My sister and I wanted desperately to return to Ferrell Street and all our friends, who were attending Woodrow

Wilson Elementary in the north of town. We had been told over the Christmas holidays that we would be moving back soon. Thanks to the measles, it turned out to be mid-February.

First

I had expected Mrs. Allison to be my teacher at Wilson. My kindergarten classmates Charlie and Sue were in her class, and I was excited about being with them again. Instead, a second first grade class was opened and I was assigned to Miss Platt's class; there were no Hiawatha Kindergarten graduates in my class. To make matters worse, Wilson first grade class was further ahead in their notebooks than I. My 16 days' measles absence meant I was seriously behind.

I enjoyed the first grade and made good progress in reading, but Miss Platt suggested supplemental reading for me over the summer.

My mother, who had been teaching such diverse subjects as world history, chemistry, science, business, math, and home economics in high schools across the Plant City area, had me read to her from the *Disney Big Golden Book of Peter Pan*.

We finished that in short order, and, as a treat, she read the original *Peter Pan and Wendy* by J. M. Barrie to me, with me occasionally trying, too. Peter and Wendy captured me completely. As a fantasy, it rested well in my small head. It was beautiful make believe.

Second

My second grade class included Charlie and Ann, from kindergarten; I felt very comfortable. Halfway through the first report period, I was reading at the second reader level, thanks to my mother's tutoring and the efforts of my teacher, Mrs. Josephine Sparkman. In a note to my parents, she wrote, "Jim is showing improvement in all his work," adding, "We are working on citizenship as he is too talkative and his hands are getting him in trouble."

Mama wrote back, "We don't understand 'his hands are getting him into trouble.'" She guessed right with the comment, "If it's fighting, I have cautioned him about it and he promised to do better."

Mrs. Sparkman and my mother didn't know that my opponent would not be appeased. I chose not to run away or tattle on Jay, my nemesis for a large part of the next two years. Mama's response to my teacher's comment about being "too talkative" was, "Yes, he is talkative, L.K. [my father] says he comes by that naturally. Ha ha."

Halloween at Wilson featured Ghost Night. I was into specters. The *Casper the Friendly Ghost* comic books were favorites of mine. The event included both outdoor and indoor activities. I was going to dress in costume, since I felt more alive in costume.

I had to choose from three options my mother presented to me: Pinocchio, Robin Hood, and an elf. Judy wanted me to go as Pinocchio, because she knew my lying ways. I chose Robin Hood; the elf was never in the running.

I was proud of my costume that Mama had sewn: the pointy shoes, the hooded top, the tights,—but mostly, the bow and imaginary arrow. At the fair, I ran with the bow slung over my shoulder, snuck quietly, pounced fiercely, and leapt nimbly, thinking I was authentically Robin-like.

When I bobbed for apples, my hood kept falling over my face, which made me laugh, along with the others watching. I shot make-believe arrows at carved pumpkins. I fearlessly touched spaghetti brains, Jell-O guts, and grape eyeballs in a darkened booth. I even sneaked a couple of eyeballs and ate them for a small, approving audience.

In the third report period, my teacher wrote, "Jim is improving slowly but steadily in his reading. Jim is always cheerful and polite."

My mother wrote back, "Jim's improvement in his reading is noticeable at home. He reads to me every evening. Jim has a keen sense of humor and loves to do for others." I was elected president of the Bird Club. Plant City was a designated bird sanctuary, but all I remember of that club was a red-headed woodpecker at work and a charm of hummingbirds darting and droning on one of our field trips.

We had naps daily in the second grade. We spread little pallets on the floor after lunch and recess. I was a lousy napper but an accomplished conversationalist.

The final report for second grade said I was "ready for the Third Reader." Mrs. Sparkman wrote generously, "Jim is a sweet, affectionate child and I have enjoyed him very much this year." My mother had written to Mrs. Sparkman earlier about my feelings for her: "He loves you very much and says, 'This teacher is the best one.'"

Me in 1955

Mrs. Sparkman recommended I do a little reading over the summer. Mama chose *A Child's Garden of Verses* by Robert Louis Stevenson, which had fantasy and more; it had rhymes like songs. She would read one of the 55 or so poems and I the next, with her prompting and helping me work out the words. The poems were innocent and honest. I got pretty good at my recitations after about 20 poems. We discussed the meaning of the poems, and Mama encouraged me to tell her how the poems made me feel. I did my best. She not only helped me improve my reading skills, but introduced me to the joys of poetry.

The Land of Nod

From breakfast on through all the day
At home among my friends I stay;
But every night I go abroad
Afar into the land of Nod.

All by myself I have to go,
With none to tell me what to do.
All alone beside the streams
And up the mountain-sides of dreams.

The strangest things are there for me,
Both things to eat and things to see
And many frightening sights abroad
Till morning in the land of Nod.

Try as I like to find the way,
I never can get back by day,
Nor can remember plain and clear
The curious music that I hear.

–from Robert Louis Stevenson's
A Child's Garden of Verses

Third

My third grade teacher, Mrs. Vivian Cook, wrote in her first
report about me, "Jim reads more fluently and he
comprehends readily . . ." She also said I was well
adjusted; she didn't know that Jay would soon insist that
we resume our fights.

In a subsequent report, she wrote, "Jim writes
exceptionally well. His self-control and good study habits
allow him spare time, which he uses profitably in the
library."

Mrs. Cook noted an improvement in my tonette playing in
pre-band class. The tonette, introduced in 1938, was a
small plastic flute that was practically indestructible. The
band consisted mostly of the end-blown flutes, with two

kids playing triangle, two on cymbals, and one on an eight-key xylophone.

I asked Mrs. Cook if I could play maracas like I had seen Desi Arnaz do on *I Love Lucy*. She laughed a good chortle, which I enjoyed. But I was serious. Our band needed some serious spicing up. Our little orchestra was as much racket as rhapsody.

In the final report period of third grade, my teacher noted, "He encourages other players to better performance on the playground. He has made good progress this year. He is a sweet child, and I have enjoyed Jim this year."

Near the end of the 1956 school year, I learned that I would advance to the fourth grade with Mrs. Ida Bender as my teacher. This was great news to me. I had known Mrs. Bender since I was a toddler, when she helped run her husband's family's small grocery next to my grandmother Zula's dress shop on Palmer Street. I went to kindergarten with her daughter, Ann, a close friend.

When Zula babysat me, I was not allowed to leave the store, except to go next door to Bender's Market for a piece of fruit. Zula would follow me out the front of the dress shop and wait on the sidewalk until I promptly returned from the market with an apple or orange I'd purchased with the nickel she had given me.

Zula didn't know that when Mrs. Bender saw me, she let me keep the nickel and gave me the fruit for the price of a hug and a peck.

On the last day of school, I decided to visit Mrs. Bender and celebrate our pending teacher-student relationship. She was sitting at her desk in the empty classroom, softly weeping. I later learned that she had been diagnosed with a serious health issue and had returned to her classroom after advising the principal, Mrs. Myrtice Clark, of her need to take a leave of absence at the start of next year's term.

I paused at the door, uncertain of what to make of the situation. I decided to go to her and, without us saying a word to each other, I climbed onto her lap and hugged her neck. She stopped crying and smiled a broad grin that only she was capable of. She kissed my cheek, set me down, thanked me, and sent me on my way with, "It's going to be just fine, Jim."

Fourth

The fourth grade started with Mrs. Raney as my teacher; she was fine. After a few weeks, Mrs. Bender returned and took over the class for the rest of the year; she was so much more than fine.

Mrs. Bender reported for the third period, "He has good comprehension in all reading material and reads voluntarily for enjoyment." In the final report to my parents, she wrote, "Jim is always pleasant and cooperative and a helpful member of his class. He will be missed at Wilson next year. I have thoroughly enjoyed Jim and his sense of humor."

Me doing early standup improv

We had lived in the Wilson Elementary neighborhood most of my life, where I had thrived and been happy. There were unpleasant times, but those times were few. Having to move temporarily because of the sinkhole next to our home was bad, but not awful. The measles were difficult, but passed soon enough.

Being bullied by my older sister and by the neighborhood bully was a challenge, but I had learned to deal with it. Jay had been my only ongoing adversary, but he never impacted my overall contentment those Wilson years.

Trick

That summer, before we moved from Ferrell Street, Judy visited our grandparents Helms. Our uncle Bobby was there and came out of the kitchen with a small bowl of ice cream. Judy asked if she could have some. Bobby was the best joke teller in the family. I idolized him. His smile was captivating. He never bullied me, although he did kid roughly.

Bobby told Judy the ice cream was a special flavor and she wouldn't like it. Judy said she'd like a spoonful to taste. He took his bowl with him back to the kitchen and came back with a tablespoon piled high with white cream. He asked my sister to open her mouth.

As she did, he shoved the spoon in and closed her lower jaw; she swallowed what she immediately knew was mayonnaise. She gagged, coughed, and nearly threw up. Bobby was laughing and laughing. Judy ran out to the front porch and cried. She never ate mayonnaise again.

Bobby and Judy, 1955

Later that day, when Judy told me about the incident, I didn't laugh or take any satisfaction in her being bullied. I feared her but was devoted to her. The prank Bobby played didn't make me love him less, but I hated what he'd done. I realized I wanted to protect Judy from him or anyone else trying to hurt her, despite her continual domination of me.

Jay'd

I hope Jay turned out okay. When I knew him, all too well, he really wasn't "okay." I didn't know what was wrong. I did know it was wrong.

I was a pretty normal kid in the second, third, and fourth grades. Wilson Elementary was a safe and nurturing setting for kids in our north Plant City community. We were all neighbors, and our parents knew each other. Fear didn't exist in our young lives. Except for Jay, I was comfortable and worry-free.

He and I fought regularly—not daily, but frequently—sometimes two days in a row. Then we'd go for weeks without incident. I never knew when we would fight next. It wasn't up to me; Jay was in charge of that. We probably had 30 fights over a three-year period. Our "matches," which happened after school, usually started over something he believed I had done or said in class.

We'd wrestle, not box. He was rather short and plump. Pinching and biting seemed to be in order for Jay. He kicked, too. I did some pinching myself, though I didn't like the idea of biting him (I was missing my front row of baby teeth then), but I kicked back. The fights normally ended with a headlock, like we had seen our pro wrestling heroes do on TV.

Jay provided an early warning in class about whether we'd fight later that day, when he complained to the teacher that I was "picking on him." His plaintive charge rarely included any specifics about what I had allegedly done. It was more a

44

call for help and support than a call to action on the part of the teacher. I was confused and stung by the accusations, and I denied them. That really upset Jay.

He ambushed me after school almost without fail if I challenged his claim that I was picking on him. What did such an ambush look like? Nothing like those that Gene Autry or Lash LaRue suffered on the big screen on Saturdays at the Capitol Theater.

No, Jay simply waited until I was on the school playground, and if I let my guard down, he ran at full speed and tackled me. Quite effective.

Based on convenience and habit, most of our matches occurred in a shallow ditch that ran directly behind the school. The little rut filled with water during rainy season, and tadpoles took over our wrestling mat. But, when dry, that was our venue. When I saw frogs beginning to appear in the ditch, I knew wrestling season was upon me.

The fights seldom lasted more than a few minutes, and neither of us was ever seriously hurt. There were a few nose bleeds, some scratches and aches, but no shiners, deep cuts, or such. Never a broken bone, although I did carry the imprint of Jay's teeth on my flesh after some of the more heated matches.

Teachers, like Mrs. Bender or Mrs. Sparkman, intervened at times, but other times they couldn't, because we quit wrestling when they approached. Our classmates neither rooted for us nor broke us up. There was no score-keeping with our matches. He won some. I won some. Some fights were draws.

Was there something wrong with Jay? I don't know for sure. Was there something wrong with me? I wasn't totally sure there wasn't.

Neither of us was stupid. I got along well with my other classmates at school. He didn't seem to fight others. I don't remember Jay having many friends, though. But neither did I know if he had enemies besides me. No one stuck up for Jay.

I thought him mean. I hated fighting with him. I wasn't scared of him, but those fights were outside my nature. He wouldn't accept our relationship as anything but hateful. I had become adept at avoiding violence by fourth grade.

My sister was a world-class bully and loved to dominate me, but not physically. An older boy on our block was also a bully, but he went no further than an occasional shove or trip. All my experience in avoiding violence didn't help with Jay. His emotions were too raw. A wrong look could light his fuse.

My family moved the summer I advanced to fifth grade. It was a move up for us to a bigger house in east Plant City. My sister and I no longer shared a bedroom. The yard had citrus and nut trees and very few stinging nettles. I started going to Stonewall Jackson Elementary, and Jay was out of my life for the next couple of years.

Although Jay and I went through high school together, our paths seldom crossed. I assume he did fine in school, but I can't really say. By then, I had a foot in height on him. We did not fight again.

The question I couldn't resolve was, "Why me?" I never figured that out. I knew I was in an irrational situation. My inability to control it was the worst part. I would come to recognize that Jay had mental health issues, an understanding that came long after grade school. It led to my forgiving him. And myself. I hope Jay turned out okay.

Toothless Me at Wilson Elementary
(second row third from left)

Shortcake

Pickin'

My first hands-on experience with strawberries was late in the second grade. My sister and her sixth grade Wilson classmates took a field trip to Cork to pick berries. My mother, who was serving as a chaperone, brought me along. Cork, "the Winter Strawberry Capital of the World," is about four miles northwest of Plant City. It consists of an elementary school and a couple of churches set in a rural landscape—and lots of strawberry fields.

Me in the mid-1950s

After a brief drive with my mother following the school bus with Judy and her class, we parked and went through the gate to the field. It was a noisy and drawn-out start. The grower and the teacher gave instructions to the kids, who each received a bucket. The teacher and several chaperones led them to the far end of the field.

The strawberry plants were laid out in rows about four feet apart, with plants every 18 inches. The rows covered the field, and the plants were loaded with plump red berry-jewels, pale green unripened fruit, and small white flowers.

My mother asked if I wanted to pick some berries. I replied, "Oh, yes, please." She went to the grower's truck and asked him for a bucket. He asked me if I knew how to pick the berries. I replied, "Not yet, sir" (I was an ever so polite child).

The grower told me they were tender and would bruise if I wasn't gentle. He cautioned me not to squeeze them as I put them in the bucket. He asked us to follow him over to the nearest plant with red berries showing.

He reached down and grasped the stem just above a berry between his forefinger and thumb and pulled down while twisting the stem. The stem was now broken about a half-inch from the berry, which rolled nicely into his hand. He took my hand and showed me how.

I dropped the first couple, but after that he released my hand and I had some success. He then helped Mama learn the same technique. She caught on quickly.

Mama thanked the grower and we set off on our "pick." I ate one and put one carefully in the bucket. Mama did the same and then began to pick with both hands, holding two or three berries before disposing of them in the pail. When we had about half a bucket, we decided that was plenty.

She asked the grower if we could keep them and he said, "Sure, enjoy," adding, "Don't wash them until just before you're ready to eat them, and they'll keep longer." She thanked him as she took me back to the car. The older kids, their teacher, and the chaperones returned soon, and we all headed back to town.

The berries we ate that evening were exceptional. As we finished our personally picked strawberries, Judy and I began to argue over who had picked the most. With her full bucket sitting on the counter, my parents and Judy decided clearly Judy had picked more. After a pause, I declared the berries I'd picked were the better tasting. No one disagreed, but Judy's face became twisted in disgust.

Misses

....

The lady's red face has a two-day straw-colored stubble beneath her fuzzy-haired crown. Her hair is a verdant green. Her scalp underneath the topknot is off-white, her hair having provided shade from the Florida sun to the young miss. She smells like caramel and is gleaming following her shower. Her name is Sweet Sensation. She is resting on top of a warm, biscuit-hued bed that is firm but springy.

Her sisters, Radiance, Winterstar, Festival, and Florida Beauty join her on the bed. They are all wet, shiny, and a bit sticky. Someone suggests sugar, so the sprinkling commences. All double-sweet and cozy now, they bathe in cream. It is poured generously over all the assembled ladies spread out across the bed. The cream has been whipped with sugar and vanilla.

The girls and the bed are now covered almost completely in the frothy cream, and they are ready to be consumed. Thus, Florida Strawberry Shortcake is conceived.

....

Strawberries are most feminine; their "stubble" is their ovaries. A berry is a fleshy fruit with no stone, produced from a single flower with one ovary. The strawberry is an aggregate accessory fruit and thus not botanically a berry. The fleshy part of a strawberry is from the receptacle that holds the ovaries, not the ovaries themselves. The supposed seeds—up to 200 and straw-colored—on the outside of a single fruit, are the ovaries of the flower, with a seed inside each ovary.

Sweet Sensation, Radiance, Winterstar, and Florida Beauty were all developed as cultivars (plant varieties produced in cultivation by selective breeding) by the University of Florida's Institute of Food and Agricultural Sciences. The Festival variety originated as a single plant in a strawberry breeding plot in Dover, Florida, and is named in honor of the Strawberry Festival in nearby Plant City.

The strawberry girls are very fertile. One strawberry plant can be picked about every three days, since the individual plant blooms are in different stages of development. As a single red fruit is picked, there are a few buds around it that can be picked in a few weeks. Approximately every 40 days, a bloom turns into a "berry," and a single plant is picked about 60 times a season. Growing season for the Florida winter strawberry is Thanksgiving to Easter. A bowl of eight or ten strawberries contains the daily requirement of vitamin C and more potassium than a banana.

Eastern Star

As a third grader, I was allowed to help at the Eastern Star's strawberry shortcake booth at the Strawberry Festival for the first time. I had been going to the Festival since I was a toddler, and this was a real honor. It was early Tuesday afternoon. I had come back from seeing the Strawberry Festival Parade in downtown Plant City with my parents. It was a superb parade.

My grandmother, Zola (Mom Foster), picked me up at my house and drove to the Masonic Temple building on Acacia Drive, just a few blocks east of the Festival grounds. A team of women there were stemming and washing fresh strawberries. I was 56 inches tall, which meant I could reach the sink. Therefore, I helped wash a few dozen berries and load a couple dozen trays of them, freshly stemmed, gleaming, and wet, into Mom's car.

Admission to the Strawberry Festival was 50 cents, but as we drove up to the side delivery entrance on Reynolds Street, we were waved in. We parked near the Parkes Main Exhibition Hall's large roll-up delivery door, where the guard welcomed us. The hall was named for Roy and Helen Parke, who were founders of Parkesdale Farms, long the leading grower in the area. The shortcake booth was just inside and to the left of the delivery entrance. For several months, the Eastern Star volunteers had been arranging the purchase of berries from local growers. The festival lasted six days in those years, with attendance around 20,000.

You smelled the strawberries before you saw them: an aromatic, slightly charred sugar fragrance. Unlike St. Clements Catholic Church's "make your own" strawberry food booth, the Eastern Star ladies prepared a paper bowl of their delicacy. The Eastern Stars insisted that their shortcake be "old fashion." It cost 35 cents.

The biscuits for the shortbread were made from scratch, and the whipped cream was never canned. Several women were whipping it by hand from an old handed-down recipe.

The Order of Eastern Star goes back to 1850 and is a Free Masonry organization accessible to women, unlike the exclusively male Masons. To join either, you had to be a Christian. The Catholic Church strongly discouraged its members from joining such secret fraternal orders. In Plant City, most members of the Order were Baptists, with a sprinkling of other Protestants.

Zola was very active in the Order and served that year as the Worthy Matron of the local chapter. The group had been running the booth for several years, and today was the busiest day.

Clearly, Zola was in charge of the booth. Everyone greeted her warmly and began asking her for instructions on their tasks and raising questions about the organization of the work. Fifteen or so women and a few men were at work inside the open-sided booth, prepping for the day and night of producing and selling thousands of shortcakes.

That day, over 700 quarts of sliced strawberries, 200 pounds of sugar, and 80 gallons of cream would be served.

Huge quantities of butter, 500 pounds of flour, and immense quantities of salt, baking powder, baking soda, shortening, and eggs were made into biscuits and baked on site. The smell of all those ingredients, mixed with the scent of strawberries and fresh cream, was scrumptious.

Men were lifting and moving bags and strawberry crates. It was the kind of production I loved—noisy, crowded, happy, and bustling—all kinds of activity with a cast of friendly people. The parade had just ended, and a crowd of some 2000 hungry customers was lined up 10–20 deep.

Putting 'Strawberry' In Festival
The strawberry shortcake booth at the Plant City Strawberry Festival and Hillsborough County Fair is always busy. Responsible for the delicious shortcake are (from left) Mary Houghton, Beulah T h a y e r, Zola Foster, Mary Shackleford, Charlsey Daniels, Pauline Powell, Rosie Miller and Pat Dillon.

Zola at the Eastern Star booth

My job was to bring two bowls of ready-made shortcake at a time to the five ladies selling the delights. After about an hour, the crush of customers eased.

My grandfather, Roy, who was also helping at the booth, asked if I wanted to join him on the midway. I said yes immediately. He checked with Zola, and she suggested we have some shortcake. We took some with us and headed to the rides, games, carnival food, and sideshows.

We went directly to the bumper cars and rode three or four times. He encouraged me to crash into him, causing cascades of laughter from both of us. He bought me some cotton candy, even though I wasn't particularly hungry following my bowl of shortcake. We attempted to knock down dolls, without success. We went on to win a plush toy fish at the ring toss.

I passed the minimum height restriction by a couple of inches, so we rode the Ferris wheel twice. On the way back to the booth, we split a funnel cake. Before going inside, we stood for some time listening to the carnie at the "Live Leprechaun—World's Smallest Man" show "call out" the crowd, trying to get them to pay a dime to see the marvel. His banter with the small group in front of the tent was funny.

The rest of my family were helping with chores at the Eastern Star booth when we returned. As we walked up, my father asked if I wanted some shortcake. I said yes. As I finished my bowl, he suggested we see the midway. I said yes again.

We started with bumper cars, and he too insisted I run into him, and we too laughed loudly. I was becoming good at crashing cars. We rode the Tilt-a-Whirl and the Ferris wheel. I got my father to stop to hear the same carnie again, and he was as amusing as before. We split a cotton candy and made our way back to the booth.

An hour or two before it closed, as the Fosters and my parents were getting ready to leave, Zola suggested shortcake. We all agreed.

Gin'd

Wreck

The accident was at the foot of a slope on Franklin Street (there are no hills in Plant City). The slope began about a block beyond Wilson Elementary, with a drop in elevation of about two feet. Kevin lived near the bottom of the slope. At the very end of the slope was a certain house.

Kevin was moaning loudly. I was silent, my eyes closed, my breathing labored. The tragic scene continued. I opened one eye slightly and squinted at her front door. We held our positions, just waiting. Our bikes were tangled together nicely. Kevin moaned louder. We waited some more, then longer.

Then, a strange woman pulled up in her car and slowed down. Her car crept past us. She stopped down the road a few yards and backed up, right by our bikes. She yelled out her window, "Are you okay?" Silence mixed with softer moans. Then she got out of her car and walked toward us, asking, "Can I help?" She was ruining it.

Kevin and I'd had the accident planned for weeks, having decided to act out our shared crush by faking a horrific bike accident. We needed the confidence of each other to implement our plan.

We'd practiced. This was our first time to perform in Gin's front yard. We just knew if we made it real enough, Gin would come out of her house and comfort us. We'd fake some major pain, and her sympathy would engulf us. It was a good plan, but this woman ruined it.

We told her we were fine, got to our feet, and rode off. She seemed surprised by our immediate, full recovery. Kevin's house was less than a block away, across Franklin Street. He parked his bike and went inside. I lived about four blocks away and also headed home. My bike was wobbly, but no permanent damage was done. We repeated this "accident" twice more before we realized that it just wasn't working and, in fact, was becoming tiresome.

Me, 4th Grade

Gin (Gina) was a classmate of ours. Kevin and I agreed that when we were around her, we felt pleasantly light-headed.

Kevin had known her longer than I had. We had moved to the north part of town from the east when I was around four. Kevin and our neighborhood pal Jerry would challenge Gin to wrestling matches when they were younger. The three of them would wrestle one-on-one, with the winner taking on the next opponent. At that early age, she matched them in physical strength and far surpassed them in intensity. She won many of her bouts.

Playboy

We moved to east Plant City, and I switched schools to
Stonewall Jackson Elementary. My fifth grade teacher,
Mrs. Bessie McGlamory (who had also been my father's
elementary school teacher), helped smooth out the
transltion, and I made new friends pretty quickly. Several
of my fifth grade classmates had attended Hiawatha
Kindergarten with me, including my loving friends Dubby,
Billy, Mitzi, Doug, and Gerry. I missed Gin mightily, though.
I was determined to stay in touch and feed my crush,
despite the several miles that separated us.

I decided to write to her. I had very little to say, being a
fifth grader. My spelling was lousy, my handwriting worse,
and, although my vocabulary was passing, I didn't have a
clue what I wanted to say. I wanted whatever I
communicated to be playful, funny, and edgy.

I was aware that *Playboy* magazine had a monthly feature
of party jokes. I liked jokes, and I liked parties. I was also
aware that the Greyhound bus station had a rack of
magazines that included "dirty magazines." I didn't know
how I could obtain a *Playboy*.

I convinced a neighborhood friend, Wally, to join me in my
new plan to win Gin's attention. We would back each
other up. We'd ride to the station on our bikes and
purchase a regular periodical like *Newsweek* and definitely
Boys' Life, an oversized magazine. We would slip a *Playboy*
into the *Boys' Life* and pay only for the *Newsweek* and
Boys' Life. We, of course, got caught. We started to put the
Playboy back, but the clerk said, "If you want the *Playboy*,
pay me for it." We put the *Newsweek* and *Boys' Life* back

on the shelf and had enough money (50 cents) for the "men's magazine." In that small cinder block station, I had moved away from silly boyhood to something like creepy prepubescent manhood.

I spent all the money I had to make that purchase and didn't have enough left to buy a three-cent stamp for my letter to Gin. I needed a workaround. Judy always seemed to have money, but I never messed with Judy. She was fierce. I mean, she scared me. I figured that when Judy was out of the house, I could sneak three pennies out of the change stash she had in her small desk and she would never miss it.

I transcribed the party jokes carefully. I didn't change a thing from the published page. I did use my own voice to start the letter and to close it. I thought all of this was clever—downright brilliant. I heard nothing after that first letter. I bought another *Playboy* the following month and wrote another letter. I hit the Judy-bank, again and again. I sent four or five monthly letters to Gin. I never heard back from her, but at least I was never caught by Judy. As my friendships at Jackson grew, I stopped trying to communicate with Gin.

I learned that when pursuing a romantic interest with a girl, it helped to have a willing co-conspirator. Over the next several years, I continued to enlist other guys (and girls) to assist me in my flirtations. I would also play accomplice for other boys chasing a crush of their own. Such cooperation felt natural and was definitely effective. I got good at it.

Dump'd

At 13, George was a growing giant. His brother David was two years younger and shorter, but much bigger. Paul, 12, was the neighborhood bully. They were together for a summer adventure. I was eight.

The three titans-to-me and I lived within three blocks of Woodrow Wilson Elementary in north Plant City. I was playing in my back yard, avoiding the stinging nettles and sandspurs, when they walked up. I asked them where they were going as they cut across my yard. "To the dump," David replied.

The back yard of our house at 1605 Farrell Street in Plant City

I asked if I could go with them. George said, "Sure." Our destination was about a half-mile north of our school. We all lived on the edge of the mostly rural small town, so after only a couple of blocks, we were in cow pastures and undeveloped property.

Our destination—we all thought—was the city dump. The three other boys were speculating loudly about what we would find. They knew something was changing at the site; I didn't. We didn't understand we were heading for an active road construction site. None of us had heard of the Interstate system.

I envisioned mounds of trash with all kinds of treasures to be found at our destination, but the "dump" had been closed and replaced by a series of highway detention basins used to control highway runoff pollution by holding rainwater temporarily during the construction of the road—Interstate 4. That Interstate was one of the first built in the country.

I really liked David and George. Paul and his bullying, not so much. He was cowed though, by Judy. She was his age but had made a living of getting him to leave me alone so she could terrorize me herself—exclusively.

We climbed a fence or two and broke through some bracken, and before us appeared an otherworldly landscape of house-size mounds of white sand.

Between the numerous mounds of bleached grit stood light turquoise ponds of water. It was breathtaking. We stood in silence at the foot of the closest dune to ponder what to do next. I got neither voice nor vote, as I recall. I didn't really want either.

We tried climbing the dune. Although it was clear that it was bulldozed, it seemed to be stable enough. We scrambled up the side, leaving a trail of footprints, and runlets of sand leaked from our heel prints. From the crest, we could see a dozen eerily tinted ponds with their accompanying blanched white dunes.

The earth around the mounds and ponds was covered in sand as well. We came down the other side of the into a flat area where the entire view was of white earth and pools of still water breaking up the brilliant scene. Overhead, the sky held scattered, fluffy white clouds set in the best of blue skies. Our vista was exceptional and required our admiration. We complied.

We climbed another dune or two, targeting the biggest or most distant ones. Some of the dunes stood back from the ponds. Others were directly by the water. We wondered if we could get closer to the water's edge.

We discussed—well, they discussed—how deep the water was. They decided, from the size of the hillocks we had just climbed, "pretty deep." We climbed a large sand pile that appeared to end at the edge of a large pond and saw a short bank along the pond's edge that would allow us to get right up to the water.

Me, age eight

As we approached the bank, someone suggested we proceed one at a time. I said since I was the smallest, I should go first. I moved forward before the other boys could react. I was at that age a bit catlike and thought I was doing my best careful-cat-sneak-up move to the water.

After about four steps, the ground gave way and I was suddenly in cold water. Completely. I popped my head out. I was a decent swimmer.

I didn't scream for help; I was with the "guys." I didn't need to yell anyway; they started moving forward. The sand started to shift under them, and large sections of sand in front of them began to cave in.

George laid his giant body on the sand by the water's edge and told Paul and David to go back up the sand pile. They did.

I swam toward George's hand, and he pulled me out quickly and cleanly. We scrambled back up the dune and sat down. I was now getting lots of questions, all in varying ways asking if I was okay. I told them I had kept my eyes shut and made sure I didn't swallow any of the water. I giggled a bit. They were much—no—abundantly relieved.

They clapped me on the back and asked other questions like, "What was it like?" "Was the water cold?" "Are you cold?" It was a warm summer afternoon, and I wasn't chilled in the least.

I never had visions of imminent death or suffered the aftershock of fear from such a close call. Once that ground was covered, we decided to head back home.

Retracing our steps through the pastures, the four of us approached the back of my house. Just as we neared the carport, my mother and Judy pulled up in our car.

I was soaking wet, but my skin didn't burn or smell funny. The guys hung back a bit as I walked up to the car. Judy was beside herself, pointing at me and laughing hysterically. She knew I'd be getting the switching of my life, and her joy was tangible. My mother climbed out of the car and hugged me tight.

Mama asked what happened, and David explained. Before he could finish, Paul slipped away and went home. The brothers told my mother that I had fallen in a pond and that they were very sorry. She said she needed to take care of me but that I appeared to be okay. She said things would be fine.

Mama, Judy, and I went inside, where I had a hot bath and got dressed. A peanut butter and jelly sandwich was waiting for me when I finished.

My pop arrived before I could finish the snack. He was not angry; he was also not impressed. I got no spanking. I didn't have to cut a switch. I didn't gain swagger either; Judy made sure of that.

But I knew those other three boys would always remember: I don't panic easily. If I wasn't a member of their gang, it wasn't because I couldn't qualify. They were just not much in my life after that day.

George finished growing at 6'10". David became a football star at Plant City High School and carried 300 pounds on a

6'8" frame. Paul gained normal size but continued to try to bully me—but not with the same vigor as before. It's as if his heart wasn't in it.

Judy picked up Paul's slack nicely. It would take several years for her to recognize what a hard-ass big sister she had been. When she was a sophomore in college, she called me out of the blue, apologizing deeply and repeatedly for the way she had treated me all of our lives.

We later talked about my escapade at the dump. She confirmed her absolute delight and thrill at seeing me dripping in the carport. We laughed together often about that day.

In 1959, 75 years after the railroad came to Plant City, the first section of I-4 was opened between Plant City and Lakeland. The dump is long gone, but its memory lives on in those of us who, as kids, ventured onto the construction site. Many young boys and girls who lived in Plant City then fondly remember playing just north of town where a major highway was taking form. It was our backyard Magic Kingdom when Walt Disney World (45 miles distant) was in the planning stages.

Part Three – Child

Christmastide

Cane'd

The two candy canes were eight inches long and two inches in diameter. The white sugar and corn syrup candies had red peppermint stripes. Unlike traditional candy canes, this pair was oversized and straight, without the standard hook on the end. They could more accurately be described as giant peppermint sticks.

Judy and I were playing with our toys from our Christmas haul on the living room floor. Our huge peppermint sticks rested next to us. It was two days after Christmas, and we had already worked our way through the shiniest and coolest gifts.

We were now looking at our new comic books. Judy had finished reading *Little Lulu*'s adventures with Tubby and Witch Hazel. I was savoring my *Casper the Friendly Ghost*. *Chip and Dale* was at my feet for my next read. We typically shared our comic book gifts with each other, if asked. I may have had to make my request a little more sweetly than Judy.

Judy reached over and grabbed my *Chip and Dale*. She stood up, crossed the floor, sat down again with her back turned to me, and began reading the newest edition about the aristocratic chipmunks, who were always ever so polite.

I liked their vaudevillian bit where approaching a doorway together, they stopped, turned to each other, and Dale said, "After you."

Chip replied, "No, no, after you."

Dale, not to be outdone: "Thank you, but I insist."

Chip, also being so formal: "Well if you insist, thank you."

Dale closed with, "No, no, thank *you*."

It may have been Judy not asking my permission, or her turning her back on me, or her starting to read my comic before I did, but I suspect it was the particular comic book taken as much as anything. These little cartoon chipmunks were very British and proper. They were kind, clever, gentle, and extra polite. It was wrong to subject them to such crude treatment as kidnapping.

I grabbed one of the peppermint sticks, walked up behind Judy, and raised it over my head with both arms, bringing it down sharply on top of her head, like Paul Bunyan chopping wood. It made a "thwacking" sound and splintered into a score of pieces. There was no blood, but Judy seemed to be paralyzed. She was holding her breath.

She finally said, "Ouch," in a hushed voice. As she dropped my comic book, she turned and made eye contact. Though I was surprised by what I had just done, she was clearly the more shocked of the two of us. Neither of us spoke.

I broke the silence with, "Give me back my book." She said nothing as she handed me *Chip and Dale*. Standing over her, I proposed we clean up the mess. We went about our labor without speaking. She was picking a few small pieces of candy cane out of her hair when I asked if I could help. She agreed. We removed the broken traces of the weapon and never reported the incident to our folks.

That was the first time I fought back directly against Judy. Previously, I had sneaked around trying to get even, or asked others for help. But I had never confronted her. She still outweighed me and was several inches taller. But I was catching up. I was not her intellectual equal, either, but again, I was making progress. She would continue to bully me, but not as often or nearly as harshly. I had learned to fight back and not let my love and fear of her fully control me.

My sister, Judy, and her pesky brother

St. Nick

Our pageants began the next year. We started practicing after Thanksgiving. Judy was the producer, director, costume designer, prop master, and narrator. I played a variety of roles and sang the lead. Staging was easy. The performance hall was my parents' bedroom, and the curtain would go up before dawn, when we knocked on their door. Our first task was to decide what to perform.

For that first year on Ferrell Street, Judy selected *A Visit from Saint Nicholas*, composed in 1823 by American poet Clement Clarke Moore. We rehearsed diligently. Diligence was my sister's permanent disposition. We practiced Christmas songs to end our performance, memorizing the lyrics. Judy had taken piano lessons and knew more about music, but I was a better singer. We stashed the props in a pillowcase we placed in the hall, along with wardrobe changes.

Christmas morning, we knocked on our parents' bedroom door. A startled, "What's wrong? Come in," was their reply. I was in pajamas, and Judy had fashioned a vintage sleeping cap that had a long tail that hung down behind me. Judy wore an oversized robe that hid her body completely.

As we entered the room, Judy began the narration with, "'Twas the night before Christmas, when all thro' the house, not a creature was stirring, not even a mouse." When she began, I held my head to one side with my eyes closed, like I was sleeping. When she said "creature," I removed my sleeping cap and pulled out two mouse ears that we had made with black construction paper. I placed them over my ears and closed my eyes like a good sleepy mouse.

Judy continued, and when she got to "sugar plums danced," I pulled two plums out of my sleeping cap and moved them like they were dancing. As Judy said, "arose such a clatter," I rushed to the hall and took two aluminum cups from the prop bag and began beating them together. With "Away to the window I flew like a flash . . .," I ran to the bedroom window and pretended to open it. As Judy read, "But a miniature sleigh and eight tiny reindeer," I went to the hall, reached in the prop case again, and drew out a die cut paper Santa's sleigh and reindeer ornament and flew it into the room with my hands.

As Judy read, "I heard on the roof the prancing and pawing of each little hoof," I quickly fetched a block of wood and a wooden spoon from the prop stash and started striking the block with the spoon as rapidly as I could. It did sound a bit like hooves. When the poem reached, "He was dress'd all in fur, from his head to his foot . . .," Judy walked to the hall and handed me the book she was using to recite the script. I picked up with, "And his clothes were all tarnish'd with ashes and soot . . .," while Judy went to the hall and picked up another pillowcase we had stuffed with some of our toys and two Christmas stockings.

As the play continued, Judy removed her robe in the hall and made her grand entrance. She had stuffed a pillow inside her red pants. She was wearing an extra-large red shirt to which we had glued cotton down the front and around the wrist of the sleeves. She was also now sporting a fake beard we had bought. She finished her costume with a pipe she'd borrowed from our father's pipe stand. It looked convincing in her bearded mouth.

As I read, "Down the chimney St. Nicholas came with a bound," she jumped into the bedroom, which quite startled our parents, but they laughed and applauded after they recovered. As I continued to read, Judy began taking toys out of the bag she had over her shoulder, putting them in the two Christmas stockings. I continued: "And giving a nod, up the chimney he rose. He sprang to his sleigh, to his team gave a whistle . . .," and Judy whistled.

We closed the poem in unison with, "Happy Christmas to all and to all a good night." Prolonged cheering and clapping ensued as we moved to the musical finale of the pageant—"Here Comes Santa Claus," followed by "Rudolf the Red Nose Reindeer." Our production closed with all four of us singing "We Wish You a Merry Christmas." We had a hit on our hands.

Scrooge

The next year, we planned a production of *A Christmas Carol* by Charles Dickens, written in 1843. It has 28,000 words, so major cuts were required. We found a copy of an old comic book that helped in writing the script. Judy played Ebenezer Scrooge, the mean and miserly lead who dominated every scene. I played Bob Cratchit, his kindly nephew who worked for him. I also took the roles of Jacob Marley, his long-dead business partner, and Tiny Tim, Cratchit's sickly son. I had multiple wardrobe changes. The trickiest one involved switching from Cratchit to Marley's ghost. My Marley stole the show with his death mask from Halloween and the long chain I had draped around my body and wound like a tail, just like in the book.

Judy and me with our best theatrical look

71

Judy and I lifted dialog, such as Bob Cratchit saying, "A Merry Christmas, Uncle! God save you!" to which Scrooge replies, "Bah! Humbug!" We relished Scrooge's indignant rant, "If I could work my will, every idiot who goes about with 'Merry Christmas' on his lips should be boiled with his own pudding and buried with a stake of holly through his heart."

The scene that stole the show was Scrooge's long-dead business partner, Marley (me) showing up as a ghost. When Scrooge first speaks to him, he tells Marley he was a good businessman. The ghost answers, "Business! Mankind was my business: charity, mercy, forbearance, and benevolence were all my business." The accompanying dialog has Marley's ghost telling Scrooge, "I am here tonight to warn you that you have yet a chance of escaping my fate." And later he adds, "You will be haunted by three spirits."

We didn't bother with portraying the three spirits. Instead, I just read summaries of their parts to Judy's Scrooge. The final scene began with Scrooge saying to Bob Cratchit, "Now I tell you what, my friend, I am not going to stand this sort of thing any longer. And therefore, I am about to raise your salary. A merry Christmas, Bob." I then removed my mustache and changed to Tiny Tim for the closing line, "God bless us everyone."

Judy and I bowed to howls of approval from our very select audience and immediately went into "Jingle Bells," "Frosty the Snowman," and the big finish, "All I Want for Christmas is My Two Front Teeth"—which I happened to be missing. Our parents sang along heartily and gave us a standing ovation at our bows.

Luke

Our final Christmas pageant was at our new home on Johnson Street. We rehearsed as diligently as before, and this time we picked the birth of Jesus from Luke 2 in the King James Version of the Bible. The stage was again our parents' bedroom, Christmas morning, before dawn. We were dressed as shepherds.

We quickly arranged a manger scene, thanks to the secret loan of Christmas decorations from our grandparents Helms. We had miniature cattle, sheep, and a horse from my own collection, a tiny manger, Joseph, Mary, and baby Jesus. Judy and I knelt by the nativity scene to read the passages.

After reading the 20-verse scripture, we broke into "It Came upon a Midnight Clear," then "Hark, the Herald Angels Sing," and finished with "Silent Night." All three annual productions played to rave reviews. Our little theater closed after "Luke."

We continued to celebrate Christmas with vigor, but those private, early Christmas morning pageants were unique to our ages and relationship for those three years. We enjoyed the whole process, but the show was the payoff. Seeing the joy, love, and amazement in our parents' faces gave both of us great happiness. Judy and I shared those feelings, even if we shared little else. We cherished our work together on our pageants, but we would rarely work in harmony together for the rest of our childhood.

Stonewall

Assessed

The psychologist told my mother that I "value emotional things more than material things." The therapist had interviewed me and my parents separately and put me through a battery of tests to evaluate me the summer after fourth grade. My family was worried about my emotional health because of all the wrestling matches I had in the fourth grade with my classmate, Jay. I wanted the fights to stop but hadn't found a way to achieve peace with him.

A picture of a "happy home" I drew as part of the psychological evaluation around my 10th birthday

We bought a new house at 807 North Johnson Street in eastern Plant City I was assured Jay could no longer seek me out to fight. However, I dreaded leaving Charlie and my other friends at Wilson. I believed I'd never have a teacher more caring than Mrs. Bender.

My parents kept telling me how wonderful it would be to have my own bedroom in a much bigger house and that General Stonewall Jackson Elementary was a fine school. I knew that several of my friends from kindergarten went there and my pal from the First Methodist Sunday school, Jimmy, went there, too. All of that helped, but I was upset about moving away from my best friend Betsy, who had been my next door neighbor since we were toddlers.

The psychologist told my mother that my "goal in life is marriage." I had assumed that Betsy would be my bride. I understood moving to a new neighborhood and attending a different school reduced the likelihood of any such outcome. I decided that upon entering Jackson, I would change my name from Jim to James as a statement on my new start in life. No one objected.

Fifth

When school opened, I learned my teacher would be Mrs. Bessie McGlamory, who eased my transition and recognized my reading skills were very good. Despite my initial reservations, my teacher reported in November 1957, "James is well liked and cheerful." She also noted that I had an excellent sense of rhythm and enjoyed folk dancing, and she complimented me on my singing voice. The note closes with, "He does not like routine jobs."

The therapist had reported to my mother in June that I was "easygoing, carefree, friendly, and good-natured with an outgoing personality who enjoys people." He also warned that I was "lazy at times, a fast worker, but not always neat."

My fifth grade class (that's me in a white sweater, last row)

That Christmas in our new house, my sister Judy and I put on a play for our parents early Christmas morning, as we had done the previous two years. After our performance, I felt things had returned to normal—perhaps even improved.

I was now in charge of my own bedroom windows. I had a respite from Judy's bad mood when she first woke up. I had my own closet that was a bit magical. It opened from my bedroom but extended to another door that opened in the kitchen. The rack closest to my room was my own, and the second rack, behind mine, was my mother's. I no longer had to wait for Judy before I could use a closet, and it was just as disorganized as I liked.

In her January 1958 report my teacher wrote, "His work habits still need improving," that I had done zero book reports, but my reading scores were excellent. In April, I had yet to do a book report. In June, my reading score was 77 out of 79, but I had not done a single book report.

My teacher's note to my mother at the end of fifth grade: "It is fortunate you have been able to teach James during his illness." (I had missed one-third of the classwork due to the flu). "You have observed that as a private pupil, he does quite well. Unfortunately, in a large group he doesn't always work." Maybe her closing comment reveals why she recommended me for the sixth grade: "James has contributed much to our music program, and I have enjoyed working with him."

Hard Ball

I became active, if not very accomplished, in Little League. I played for the Coca Cola Redskins. I played any position that didn't require throwing, catching, or running. I was something less than mediocre at bat but loved being on a team and could set my jaw just right to look like a serious threat. I enjoyed playing the game, in spite of my poor skills and little talent. My poor performance didn't interfere with my enthusiasm. I disliked practice and only did the minimum, but actually playing a game was exciting.

**The 1957 Plant City Coca Cola Redskins
(I'm kneeling, second from left, with scowl)**

It was more than the visual element of balls flying into the air or bouncing on the ground, people running around a diamond-shaped infield, or a teammate shagging a fly ball. It was the smell of leather gloves, freshly mowed grass, hot dogs grilling, and popcorn popping. The sound of a bat striking a ball, the smack of a pitch sharply thrown into a glove, a cheer from the crowd after an outstanding play, and the complaints of parents at bad calls were all captivating.

The baseball itself felt luxurous with its horsehide skin and two rows of protruding laced sutures in red and black. The dirt around the infield was gritty. I loved how the freshly washed cotton uniforms that were starched but soft and the way the tapered bat's knob fit snugly in the hands. I thought baseball was the perfect game, and that would not change.

Homebound

The psychologist included in his report that "the mother seems to have a leading role in the family, mother and father have completely different personalities—father has a 'doesn't care attitude,' mother has strong temperment and is inclined to worry about responsibilities." He said he believed I was more like my mother than my father.

Me and Mama, c. 1958

Mama began her masters program in special education at Florida Southern College the summer between my fifth and sixth grades.

I found myself drawn to several of her college textbooks—particularly the volume on world religions. I rarely studied a book. I enjoyed reading and took some pride in my comprehension and retention abilities. I almost never read the same passage twice. This book was different. It held concepts new to me. I preferred concepts to details, and the book left me wanting to dig deeper. I went back and reread the same section on a subject to fully grasp its fit or discordance with similar subjects in a different religion. I found the exercise in contrast powerfully fulfilling.

Mama had decided to enter the home-bound teaching program. She would leave the classroom at Turkey Creek and teach K–12 children who were physically unable to attend traditional school. She had students who were blind, injured, or ill. Her territory would be from Fort Lonesome, north to the county line and from Keysville, west to Seffner. That meant a lot of driving, which severely aggravated the neck pain she had started suffering years before, when we lived temporarily with her parents.

Judy was then in ninth grade. She was smart and worked hard at her studies. She had always received outstanding reports in elementary school. The results of an IQ test she took showed her to be more intelligent than 90 percent of her age group. Her grades reflected her academic effort—in seventh, eighth, and ninth grades, she was an honor student, with all As and Bs. I was having no such success in school. My IQ test results showed a score higher than

Judy's, which was a shock to my family, but I wouldn't learn about this for several years.

Sixth

In the sixth grade, I did commendable work, except in "self discipline." My first male teacher, Paul Woods, wrote in an April 1958 grade report that I was continuing to do good work in my daily assignments, but "James' problem is talking too much in the classroom." I had been elected class president, but it was a mixed class of 12 fifth graders and 12 sixth graders. My competition was limited, and I talked to everyone—a lot, evidently.

Late in the school year, Mr. Woods had the class do a project making a mural in conjunction with our reading, geography, and social studies classes. The mural was a view of the terraced adobe pueblo in Taos, New Mexico. I was very engaged in the effort. I drew the prickly pear cacti, which I thought the most compelling part of the image. As we completed the mural, Mr. Woods told us he would include a section on cacti in an upcoming lesson plan. I was excited and told Mama of my growing interest in the plant I found strange and thorny but magnetic.

Mama arranged a Saturday afternoon visit to a home in Tampa with a large garden dedicated to cacti. The couple who owned the home were renowned for the wide variety of cacti on display and were recognized as experts on the spiny plant. There, I absorbed as much information as I could. The owners gave us a private tour that was both scientific and bewitching. Several varieties of cacti were in bloom. The couple explained in great detail how the cactus survived in the hostile desert environment, and I found it new and gripping; I even took notes that I'd study later—which was out of character for me.

Later that week, Mr. Woods presented his lesson on cacti. My mind soon drifted off to observe what was happening outside the bank of windows to my left. I was sitting next to my good pal Doug Smith and tried to strike up a whispering conversation. Doug stopped me and said he wanted to hear Mr. Woods. I turned my attention back to him as he was talking about how cacti absorb water in the driest of climates because their roots extend so far down to find water.

I knew that was wrong. The couple with the cactus garden had explained that even as it begins to rain in the desert, the cacti shoot out more roots so that the plant becomes more hydrated than the soil it's growing in.

I raised my hand, and Mr. Woods called on me. "Mr. Woods, what you just said isn't true." I hadn't intended to put him on the spot, but I did. He asked what I meant. "The root systems of American cacti go out, not down." He paused and asked why I thought so. "I saw it myself," I answered. He suggested we discuss it later.

Despite my deep respect for him, I couldn't stop myself. "You need to correct the part about tap roots going down to find water, that's not how it works." He paused, longer this time, and, with a touch of frustration in his voice and face said, "James, why don't you go to the library and research the question and come back with a report on what you find." I was surprised, but ready to take the challenge. I was confident in my knowledge and upset about the misinformation.

**My 6th grade class, Stonewall Jackson Elementary
(me in last row, second from right)**

I went to the small school library in the main building and found a few books on cacti. Two of them were explicit about cactus roots spreading out around the plant. Both books had drawings of the root system. I didn't linger in the library or take detours back to my temporary classroom building as I normally would. Instead, I checked out both books and went directly back to class. I quietly took my seat. As Mr. Woods completed his lecture on cacti, he asked me to present my findings to the class. I was ready.

I gave a summary of the root system described in the two sources without reading the material aloud. I then handed the two books to Mr. Woods. The books were open to the drawings of the plants' roots.

Mr. Woods studied it briefly and said, "Thank you, James. You were absoulutely correct, and thank you for correcting me." He handed the books to two classmates and asked them to pass them on. I was amazed, because at age 11,

I knew I had likely crossed a line with one of the best teachers I ever had. He wasn't angry or embarassed, and he appreciated my righting the record. Following the cactus incident, I recognized that misinformation was intolerable to me, unless it was part of a gag that everyone understood to be humourous or thought-provoking.

Something was triggered in that cactus episode. For the next year or so, I was a serious student. I memorized all the bones in the human body, took advanced math classes in junior high school, and read for pleasure dozens of science fiction works by Asimov, Bradbury, Heinlein, and Clarke.

The final comments from my psychologist were that I had "strong convictions" and was "very secure," with a "good sense of responsibility." The last comment Mama recorded was, "Child not independent, but becoming more so." The psychologist's observations about me largely held true.

Insurrectionist

I was proud to be at a school named for such a magnificient Confederate General; I believed him to be the most gallant of Dixie's generals—having died on the front line of a battle.

My father's great grandfather, Cyrus Newton Helms, had fought for the South in the Civil War as a private in the Army of the Potomac, Alabama 5th Regiment, Company A, the "Barbour Grays." He saw battle at the Seige of Yorktown, the Battle of Seven Pines, Malvern Hill, and Sharpsburg (Antietam) in 1862, and the Wilderness in

1864. His presence at Antietam is significant—it was the bloodiest battle of the Civil War and of any single day in all of U.S. history. Cyrus joined the army at age 17. I suspect I would have followed Cyrus' example had I lived in Alabama in his time.

My mother's great grandfather, Renny Martindale, served between 1862 and 1865 with the Kansas 12th Infantry, Company F, as a corporal. His unit saw battle in Kansas against the guerilla war the Rebels were waging and later action in Arkansas. Were I to have been in Kansas in 1862, of fighting age, it is likely I too would have served in the cause of the Union.

My great great grandfather Renny Martindale

As I matured, an unexpected and building emotional response in me took form that made me think further about those who take boundless pride in a failed effort to break up the United States.

Dress Shop

Fitting

....

I'm in my customary spot—sitting on my favorite stool in the changing room, flipping through this month's *Vogue*. *Harper's Bazaar*, *Glamour*, and *Women's Wear Daily* are nearby. The three mirrors around me are floor-length and spotless. I hear the muffled voice of Mom Helms, my grandmother, through the drawn curtain. I can faintly hear her asking, "Why don't you try it on?" These words are a constant theme for me in my early years.

It's time to exit the dressing room. I exchange the *Vogue* for *Glamour* and sit at my grandparents' desk in the main store to further examine the latest fashions. I smile and say good afternoon to Patsy Ambrose's grandmother, Mrs. Chiles. She is with a much younger friend, who takes an Ellen Kaye white drop-waist garment into the dressing room.

**Mom Helms in her early 40s,
about the time she opened her dress shop**

Patsy's grandparents and my grandparents are close friends. The two couples play bridge regularly on Mom Helms' porch. I don't know Mrs. Chiles' friend, but she's made a fine selection—a white garment with tiny yellow and green daisies spread across the full-skirted dress. There is a large bow at the waist and rhinestones in the center of some of the daises. Mom Helms walks behind the desk and pats me on the shoulder as she enters the dressing room and closes the curtain. I have no doubt she will make the sale, as Mrs. Chiles' friend returns looking lovely and pleased in her spring finest. Mrs. Chiles is beaming.

....

The Shop

My grandfather, Lem, had been the breadwinner as a meat cutter and then an operator of a small retail store selling milk, ice cream, and soda on Reynolds Street. Zula was a homemaker. Most women in that era were housewives. Those who did have a profession were teachers or nurses, but Zula pursued a different path— retail. She decided she wanted to open her own business.

With Lem's support, she opened Helms Dress Shop, Inc., at 104 Palmer Street in 1936, during the worst of the Great Depression. She would say she opened the shop with "a dollar and a prayer." She also brought expansive enthusiasm. She loved to sell and soon became an accomplished merchandiser. She was the only stockholder, but not a director of the corporation. Her husband and sons held the officer positions. Lem, who kept the books, was indispensable, bolstering Zula and assisting her as needed. She would say of him, "The finest man I ever knew."

As a toddler, I was a frequent visitor to the dress shop, where Lem and Zula babysat me. Well before I could read, I looked at ladies' fashion magazines for entertainment. The four-color pictures were spectacular, and I liked the slick, fancy feel of them. The dresses, worn by stunning, confident women, enchanted me.

I also liked the feel of the store, with two racks of dresses in a full spectrum of colors and a variety of styles. The racks extended the full length of the store's walls, and assorted sales racks made up the middle aisle.

The two mannequins in the store display window changed clothes with the seasons a bit ahead of the women of Plant City. There were shelves of hats with feathers, nets, and flowers and rows of gloves in fancy boxes in a glass display case. The dress shop was a tapestry of color and fabrics. It would thrive for well over 30 years and comfortably support the couple's family of three boys.

The action in the store was fascinating. I knew many of Zula's customers, like Mrs. Chiles, and almost everyone was friendly. I found it delightful to see a woman go into the dressing room looking apprehensive and return sunshiny in a new frock that flattered her.

Zula did not hesitate to let a shopper know she had selected the wrong dress. She was quick to recommend a series of dress options to her customers that fit their body shape, age, and personality and were appropriate for the intended use of the item. Her fashion sense was unerring, and she was a true sales professional, answering questions and fetching items. She always sought to insure that what her customers bought would look good on them and that others would notice.

She handled the salesmen (yes, always men) who visited the shop to pitch a new line of clothing differently. Clearly, she was in the ascendant position with them. She instructed them to make appointments outside of normal business hours. Those who ignored her request were subject to her ire. Her transformation from accommodating salesperson to businesswoman with limited time for an unscheduled sales pitch was remarkable. She was never rude, but she was firm with them. If a salesman happened to appear while she was attending a customer, she kept a razor-sharp focus on the client. The salesman would have to wait to get her attention.

Zula in front of the hat section and Lem behind the lingerie and gloves display case

Zula was born in wiregrass country, in Ozark, Alabama. Her mother died in childbirth, and she was raised by her father, Simeon Garner, and his sister, Louisa Garner (Aunt Lou). She moved in the 1920s to Plant City after she married my grandfather. She was not destined to be a country girl or a small town girl. She was a serious merchandiser and successful businesswoman with an artist's sense of symmetry and color. Her vision for the store was to sell ladies' ready-to-wear in all the well-known brands. "While dresses and other apparel will be exclusive, they will not be expensive."

Every few years, Zula and Lem took the train to New York City to visit the Garment District. There, they examined, first hand, the latest fashions and decided which dresses to buy wholesale for her store. The heart of the 15-block District was between West 39th and 40th on Seventh Avenue. Ninety percent of all garments made in United States came from the District.

The couple saw truckloads of cloth going into the dressmaking houses and finished garments coming out. Racks of dresses were pushed along the sidewalks in a scramble. Tens of thousands of skilled drapers, dressmakers, patternmakers, embroiderers, glovers, leatherworkers, milliners, and seamstresses flooded the streets of the District at lunch every weekday, joined by an army of laborers, executives, secretaries, and accountants and occasionally a short, fierce, steely blue-eyed businesswoman from a small southern town in Florida.

Zula understood her market. She sold reasonably priced, fashionable women's ready-to-wear in a town of eight or nine thousand. She avoided selecting multiple dresses in the same style and fabric so that two women customers of hers meeting on the street wouldn't be wearing the same dress. She employed a highly skilled alterations seamstress, Mrs. Tyler, who could remake customers' selections to fit, which permitted her to limit the array of dress sizes in the racks.

Zula's Home

Zula exhibited her instinctive sense of style at home, too. In 1942, for $4,500, she and Lem purchased a three-bedroom, two-bath Florida bungalow built in 1921. It was known as the J. W. Booth House. Its exterior featured a galvanized metal shingle roof and forest green-stained heart of cypress siding. The roof shingles were coated with zinc to keep them from rusting. Cypress is a long-lasting wood and, when stained or painted properly, can last hundreds of years. It is resistant to rot and insects. The house was designed to be permanent.

305 North Howard Street in the 1940s

The wood frame house featured a covered screened front porch with doors leading to Baker Street on one side and the large grassy space of the double lot on the other. All accents to the verdant-stained structure were painted a creamy hue—from the external window frames to the porch's brick posts and two brick chimneys that extended to the second-floor roof, providing a cloud-like juxtaposition to the tree-like aspect of the siding. Matching art deco planters sat atop brick pedestals on both sides of the porch. The neatly trimmed six-foot azaleas that fronted the house provided privacy.

The interior was streamlined, geometric, and colorful. The walls had crown molding and ten-foot plaster ceilings. A parlor with a brick fireplace featured an art deco mantle clock that look liked Napoleon's hat and chimed liked Big Ben in London. The wood floors were always polished. The furniture was understated but stylish. The living room featured a walnut upright piano, and the walls were adorned with colorful Audubon bird prints professionally framed and matted.

As fondly as I remember the house and the inside, the outside was the most evocative. A cast concrete bird feeder (also cream-colored) in the back yard was heavily trafficked by various families of song birds. Seven mature live oaks ranged along the Baker and Howard Street sidewalk. Dogwoods that Lem had transplanted from Alabama lined the back of the property and bloomed in champagne and pink annually. Three 40-foot Mexican fan palm trees lined the inner yard along the concrete driveway, leading to a garage made of cypress shingles stained to match the house.

Lem was an accomplished landscaper who, with Evert Smith, an African American gardener, designed and maintained the yard, with its magnolia tree, dogwoods, oaks, citrus trees, and white, red, and purple azaleas.

The fence symbolizes Zula to me. In a very early picture, I am holding onto the galvanized pipe that runs near the top of the art deco chain wire ornamental fencing. It has a twisted wire pattern from the pipe to the ground, and along the top, arches break the linear pattern into a pleasing flowing design.

The fence enveloping the yard embodied Zula's refined, easy grace. It had an ornamental nature, without pretense to utility. I admired it and couldn't resist touching it often. It impressed on me that once a necessary function is performed (as at Zula's home and in her business) graceful adornment makes the effort more worthwhile and fulfilling.

We celebrated all of my early birthdays in Zula and Lem's large yard, thick with St. Augustine grass (stinging nettles, sandspurs, and gopher holes were unacceptable to Lem). The homes my immediate family lived in, and our yards, were not big enough to host a dozen kids for such parties. Next to the fence in the front yard, an irrigation spigot protruded from the ground a couple of feet; it was a perfect water fountain for me and my guests at the parties.

The art deco chain wire fence with child's water fountain

Gilchrist

Gilchrist Park was the nexus of my youth. I started coming to the park as a very young child, beginning with an Easter egg hunt soon after I began to talk. After we moved to Ferrell Street, our family continued to go the Easter egg hunt at Gilchrist after our private one at home.

Me finding eggs at Ferrell Street

As a result of scoring eggs at Gilchrist, I developed a taste for hard-boiled eggs. The colors were lovely and striking, but I rather preferred to eat them than hoard them in a basket. They're good without any seasoning, but a little pepper or salt makes them a perfect treat.

A 20-foot in diameter pine-covered oval band shell sat on the Knight Street side of the park. It was very old, and I thought it a remnant of the previous century. It was there when I was an infant and when my family bought a home on Johnson Street in 1959, a block east of the park. I don't recall seeing any concerts there, but I do remember a few speeches completely unworthy of comment. I also recall finding a trove of tinted eggs at its base several Easters in a row. Now, that was memorable.

I had to walk or bike past Gilchrist daily on my way to grade school and then to junior high. I knew the park well and observed each fallen tree, remodel, and addition. I inspected the new landscaping that was installed seasonally and monitored its progress.

Chief

....

I go to Gilchrist Park frequently since sixth grade ended a few weeks ago. I watch the shuffleboard matches from the wooden benches ringing the green-painted cement playing area with its painted white lines. It is free entertainment, and I look forward to going there.

There are 12 courts at Gilchrist, which, in the mid-morning, are occupied by old men who all appear to know each other. Women and younger folks are rarely seen around the courts. One team consisting of two players challenges another team of two, and they stand at opposite ends of the 39' x 6' court.

The proper name of the game is "deck shuffleboard," from its frequent appearance on cruise ships. It is a game of skill. There is a nice color, sound, and movement to the game. The pucks, or discs, are four red, four black. The scoring zone is painted white, and the contrast between the emerald court surface, the brilliant white of the scoring zone, and the position of the red and black discs is dazzling under the Florida summer sun. The men use pushing cues to send the pucks down the court in either offensive or defensive strategies. The waxed pucks "whoosh" across the court, sometimes with fierce briskness and sometimes with measured sluggishness; when pucks collide, an unmistakable slapping "whack" echoes through the park. The better players are able to block and hide their discs behind other discs.

There is considerable excitement in the game. The old guys needle each other and exclaim their losses and good shots. The chatter on the court, however, is unlike any I've heard before. Many of the men are World War I vets, and their talk is of the Great Depression, movies and stars I've never heard of, Prohibition, and obscure places and battles.

I have been admonished by several of the old players for trying to talk to them, even after their matches. But Chief and Mr. Tony don't mind at all if I talk to them, even in the middle of play.

Chief is perhaps the best and most easygoing player at Gilchrist. He wears a permanent smile under his "Navy" baseball cap. He served on the USS Roanoke during the North Sea Mine Barrage. I've never heard of that battle. Chief says his mine-laying ship was based in Inverness, Scotland, for six months at the close of "The War to End All Wars." He says the ship's mission was to slow down U-boat movements from Germany to the Atlantic shipping lanes. He tells me, "At the time, it was the biggest mine-planting stunt in the world's history." His stories are full of interesting mates and places and are always sprinkled with laughter.

A creepy guy named Mr. Ernie has started joining my chats with Chief and Mr. Tony. His daily uniform is plaid Bermuda shorts and a white tank top. His skin is wrinkled and saggy. He offers little to the conversation. When he speaks, he is generally negative in tone and off point. He doesn't laugh. He sits next to me on the bench and begins "geggin' in" on my talk with Chief and Mr. Tony.

Just after Chief and Mr. Tony win a hard-fought match, Chief comes over and says he wants to talk to me. He motions for me to follow him to a nearby picnic table, and we sit down across from each other. Chief says, "James, not everyone here is your friend. Mr. Ernie is a bad guy, and you should never be alone with him." I start to interrupt with a question, but Chief puts his index finger to his mouth and hushes me.

"James, I like you, but I think you're spending too much time with us old guys," he says quietly. I tell him that I enjoy watching shuffleboard and hearing stories from him and others.

"James, I'm asking you to stop coming by here and find other things to do." I am shocked, but I know that Chief is probably right. Mr. Ernie is disturbing, and none of the other men, including Chief, is really a pal. "Yes, sir," I reply and we shake hands warmly.

I still ride by the shuffleboard courts on my bike but I don't stop. I see the bearish Mr. Tony and hear his gruff laugh as Chief tells another yarn of the high seas. We even wave to each other sometimes.

....

Joy Box

Soon after my friendship with Chief ended, I was riding my bike home from Stonewall Jackson Elementary, a couple blocks west of the park on Gilchrist Street, and pulled up to the drainage canal near the shuffleboard courts. I was in a particularly good mood, for no reason at all. The canal ran through the park from the southwest to the northeast to Tomlin Street.

There was always a steady, meandering flow of water going north through the open 10-foot wide, 6-foot deep canal. A food processing plant was located upstream from the canal, and its waste formed chunks of grayish, fuzzy sludge that floated on the surface. It was without odor, and the sight struck me as fanciful rather than repulsive. I wanted to remember that scene and how I felt at that moment forever. I wanted to capture the sense of being alive and aware of my existence. I had never attempted that previously and didn't know if it would work, but I wanted to try.

The canal through Gilchrist Park

I closed my eyes for a second and said to myself, "I will always hold on to this moment." I opened my eyes. I could still see the image that I had locked in. I started home, and on the way, I could see in my mind the exact image that I had promised to retain, along with the feeling of contentment I had by the canal. That night, while watching television, I pulled up the picture I had taken mentally of the canal with the associated emotion. I did the same the next day. A week later, I was successful again. Months later, I tried again and was successful.

I had captured the instant of carefree delight looking at the canal. The scene itself was unremarkable. It was of no great beauty, and nothing noteworthy had happened while I looked at the canal. But I'd permanently preserved my sense of peace in that moment. I didn't want to remember an event or an action. I wanted to prove to myself that when I tried, I could create a lasting memory of the pleasure of life itself.

At that age I had countless "joy boxes" in my mind. They were filled with memories of loved ones, friends, happy activities, and events and things that gave me joy. Whenever I needed cheering up, I could open one of these boxes and relief would follow. But this time I had intentionally constructed a "joy box" on my own, allowing me to retain the memory of that instant at Gilchrist Park. It is available for full recall and gives me immediate comfort.

Pigskin

From my earliest days, I loved football. Football ruled in the Gilchrist Park area for boys in the early 1960s. There were four private football venues within an easy bike ride of my house. The games were arranged at school and usually took place on the weekend. They lasted a couple of hours and included five or six players on a side. Bathrooms and water were always available in the host boy's home adjoining the football field/yard.

Me on Christmas morning 1951, with new football uniform and pistol (I was too short for the shotgun)

We played most of our football games at Gerry's house on Knight Street across from the Park. His house sat on a double lot, and the yard on the north side of his home had room for a game of tackle or touch. I was somewhat better at football than baseball. I wasn't picked first or last. I enjoyed football for the exercise, the impact of the clash, and the scramble, although I preferred the grace of baseball.

Over a dozen regulars could be counted on to show up. Rat Ward was probably the best athlete on the field; he was a decent quarterback, an even better receiver, and the best defense player. Dubby was a solid player, with Tommy close behind. My two best friends, "Spruce" and Keller, were almost always there.

Me and Kenny

Our other football fields were at Rat's, Jimmy's, and Dubby's houses. Dubby, who had attended Hiawatha Kindergarten with me, lived across from the park. His house had all the best new features, like heated floors and air conditioning. He could draw better than any boy my age. He was a good athlete, and I never tired of losing to him when we played basketball on his driveway backboard. He was even more dominant at table tennis, which we played in a screened shed behind his house. He slaughtered me on the public tennis courts in west Plant City, too. I won just often enough to retain a slight ember of hope of winning again, so I was almost always good for another go. I was persistent, it seems, in enjoying the game, if not in celebrating a victory.

Gilchrist Park survived. Albert W. Gilchrist was the 20th governor of Florida. He made his fortune as a citrus grower and donated land to Plant City for public use. He left much of his fortune to orphans and needy children. The legacy of his charity is confirmed with the playful screams of each child that enjoyed his park.

Crickets

Sleepless

....

I toss toward the oscillating fan, turn on my back and flip the pillow to the cooler side, then toss toward the three open windows abutting the long side of my bed. It doesn't work; I can't get to sleep. The male crickets are cranking out their all-and every-night-long chirps. Their calls coming in through the large windows next to my bed and the two smaller windows above my head don't help my insomnia.

The boisterous field crickets (*Gryllus rubens*) within three feet of my bed are aggravating and relentless; our block is loaded with them. On a muggy, still summer night, our metal-roofed house has soaked up the high Florida sun's heat all day, and the crickets compound the oppressive heat. The canopy of the 30-foot live oak sheltering my bedroom captures and holds the heat and the cricket concert. They do make good bait for bluegill or shellcrackers, and cardinals love them, but I don't.

Other noises prevent a summer's sleep. My bedroom is next to the back porch, with its sloped metal roof sitting as an easy target under a mature pecan tree. In summer, the pecans are still green, but their shells are hard. Squirrels love the unripened nuts and gnaw them off the tree, have a taste, and drop them to the roof. A nut hitting the porch is loud enough to end deep slumber—it is less "ping" and more "thwack." The pecan then bounces a couple of times with a "rap, rap" and slides off the roof. It demands I listen to the entire show, which ends with a "smish" upon striking the ground.

Then there's the stray mosquito. *Culex nigripalpus* is a freshwater mosquito ranging from the southeastern United States, across the Caribbean, Central America, and northern South America. It's not the bite that keeps me awake, or even the fear of disease that could follow a bite. It's the buzz: exasperation in flight.

I have learned to sleep with a Black Flag spray can at the ready. If I forget the sprayer, I have to turn on the light to find and chase the blood suckers—completely waking me up. I get so good with my Black Flag gun with the lights off, I can track a flying mosquito from bed and get it cold without sitting up.

Having grown up in a train town, the never-ending sound of trains rolling through town or coupling at the yard at Calhoun Street, only a half mile away, is "white noise" to me. Hammering comes from Plant City Steel Corporation (one mile away) as the overnight shift rushes to fabricate large rocket boosters for Cape Canaveral. It should be a nuisance, but when a huge metal rocket casing is beaten, it sounds like the toll of a giant bell in D Major—it has a "pong" sound that is unmistakable. Although the "chiming" is irregular, it becomes peaceful as its strikes echo across Plant City. No, it is the suffocating heat with help from the singing crickets that keeps me awake.

....

Wafting Hymns

....

Beginning late in the summer of 1960, I get relief from my heat-induced wakefulness. As I stretch out on my bed after sprinkling some more water on my neck, arms, and legs and adjusting the fan, I hear bass notes and voices; it is a *Homo sapiens* choir rather than *Gryllidae*. A human choir is a collective harmonious voice seeking to please an audience, while a cricket choir is individual voices, all singing their individual parts at the same time, seeking supremacy to procreate with its audience. I prefer the human kind.

Such human sounds have never before drifted through my open windows. A choir is singing, along with an organ and a drum, to a jumpy tune I can't identify and lyrics I can't make out, but the music is captivating. I forget to listen to the crickets' chorus. It is after 11 p.m., and I can't imagine where the music originates; I drift off to the mystery choir's serenade.

Next morning, I ask my family if they too heard choral music. They did not. I ride my bike to Kenny's house and ask him. He says he has no idea and suggests we ask his dad. We go to Mr. Keller's electrical shop, and he says there is a gospel tent revival going on "across the tracks," meaning where black families live, about a mile from my house. I know immediately that's it. The previous night I had my first extended taste of live black spiritual music. Not only did I enjoy it, it was a wonderful antidote to heat, crickets, and sleeplessness. I need more of that.

The tent revival has a limited, one-week run. I hear the music again on two nights due to a favorable wind. I go to sleep both nights without the temperature or cricket choir distracting me. I know when the revival stops I have to find an alternative.

There Is an AM radio in my room, but an even better one in the attic. I help myself to it and remove the speaker from my cheap one and wire it into the upgraded one. I place the radio with its speaker appendage next to my bed. It doesn't add a lot of fidelity, but it does create a bit of "oomph." I begin searching for black gospel music after 11 p.m.

The first meaningful communication I ever receive from the community of "colored town" offers a taste of something unfamiliar yet comfortable, stirring yet soothing, spiritual in a way I didn't know existed. I am familiar with the hymns of the Methodist Church, having sung them weekly as part of the choir. I am familiar with Charles Wesley, an early leader of the English Methodist Church, who wrote around 6,000 hymns, including *Hark the Herald Angels Sing*. His elegant poetry moves me to think and worship, and the melodies are uplifting.

"I Want a Principle Within"
Words: Charles Wesley, 1749

Almighty God of truth and love,
to me thy power impart;
the mountain from my soul remove,
the hardness from my heart.

O may the least omission pain
my reawakened soul,
and drive me to that blood again,
which makes the wounded whole.

But black gospel is much more urgent, its voice rawer and more powerful. I find myself not just moved, but touched personally by the authentic vernacular of the lyrics, the force of the beat, and the hypnotic effect of a spiritual phrase, often sung by one person, followed by a direct response or comment, often by many voices—God's love appearing in a different and welcoming aspect to me.

"His Eye is on the Sparrow"
Traditional Negro Spiritual

"Let not your heart be troubled"
His tender word I hear
And resting on His goodness
I lose my doubts and fears
Tho' by the path He leadeth
But one step I may see
His eye is on the sparrow
And I know He watches me
His eye is on the sparrow
And I know He watches me

I begin searching for black gospel music on my radio on a Sunday night. Early on, I stumble on WLAC in Nashville, Tennessee. The Nashville station is one of a handful of "clear channel" stations that can be heard across large sections of the southern United States.

A white disc jockey, John R. (John Richbourg), plays record after record of African American gospel. I drift off quickly that night to "If You Just Keep Still," sung by Mahalia Jackson, including the fine line, "Many nights I lay in torment"; it is the best sleep of the summer. I know Mahalia was speaking of a tormented soul and not my insomnia, which is temporary and simply uncomfortable. The pain that comes through her voice is powerful and melodically compelling.

I have Sundays covered and sleep peaceably those nights. I become familiar with such songs as the rocking call and response of "Wade in the Water" by Ella Jenkins, the somber and inspirational "Take My Hand, Precious Lord" by the 14-year old Aretha Franklin, and the operatic "We Are Climbing Jacob's Ladder" by Paul Robeson.

The more black spiritual songs I hear, the better I understand in Plant City there is suffering I hadn't known existed and is rarely discussed in my own community. I begin to sense that "race music" reveals permanent and deep hurt in the lives of many of my African American neighbors, even though I am isolated from it.

Me in late 1959

As school starts, I have four speakers wired to my new radio; there are now no other operating radios in our house. I listen to WLAC on the other six nights of the week, and I find that secular rhythm and blues has a similar effect on my ability to ignore cricket choirs and the dismal heat.

WLAC has black listeners across much of the U.S. listening to Mississippi Delta blues, available nowhere else on the long-range, nighttime radio dial. There are commercials for products like Royal Crown Hair Pomade and Randy's Record Shop, a mail-order phonograph record company out of Gallatin, Tennessee. Some of the ads include sexually suggestive double entendres, which, as a preteen, I find entertaining and daring.

Some brilliant blues records are spun on that broadcast, such as Jimmy Reed's earthy "Ain't That Lovin' You Baby" (with the lyric, "I'll tell ya what I would do: I would rob, steal, kill somebody just ta get back home ta you. Ain't that lovin' ya, baby?"), Howlin' Wolf's rocking harmonica riffs in "I've Been Abused" ("I feel so bad, this ain't gonna last; I've been scorned, and I've been kicked out"), Robert Johnson's thumb-picked thumping "Stones in My Passway" ("I got stones in my passway and all my roads seem dark at night"), John Lee Hooker's sorrowful "No Shoes" ("No shoes on my feet, and no food to go on my table. Oh, no, too sad, children crying for bread"). These songs speak of things I've never heard sung about before. I am learning a new language that is full of soul.

I have known Ray Charles music for years, and my entire family loves him. Elvis, of course, covered lots of "race records" successfully and well. But with the addition of Little Richard, Fats Domino, James Brown, Ruth Brown, Bo Diddly, Jackie Wilson, and Chuck Berry to my list of favorite musicians, I want my own library of soulful music. We bought a hi-fi console a couple of years earlier, and my parents have been purchasing "long-playing" 33 1/3 rpm records of their favorite big band groups. My sister and I start purchasing our own—of pop favorites like Elvis, the Everly Brothers, and Johnny Mathis as well as soul singers. James Brown's "Please, Please, Please" is my first purchase, followed quickly by the album *Ray Charles* and Jackie Wilson's *He's So Fine*.

I play these and other soul albums over and over. Pop comes home from work one late afternoon when I am in the living room doing my best John R. imitation. I repeat individual songs several times as only a compulsive preteen can. Pop must tire of my act.

We discuss "Negro" music. He starts by saying he really doesn't like "the Godfather of Soul" and the Famous Flames' version of "Try Me"—my favorite. He asks me why I like it. I reply, "It makes me happy."

He declares forcefully, "If it makes you so happy, why don't you go live with them." I am shocked by the harshness of his comment; his nature is consistently kind and loving. He and I both know "going to live with them" is impossible, given my age and the reality of life in Plant City.

I don't reply; I turn off the hi-fi and go to my room. I listen to John R. that night and quickly enter a deep sleep.

....

Part Four – Youth

Dress Shoppin'

Opening Scene

....

"Why don't you try it on?" This question always begins the show. My grandmother, Zola—Mom Foster—is the first to perform. She enters the closest empty changing room with three garments she's selected from the racks of the Boulevard Collection on the Floor of Fashion at Maas Brothers in Tampa. She hopes they will project "natty."

I sit comfortably in my regular position with my back against the gray, overstuffed bench. I watch the rest of the cast—my great aunt Aletha and my mama, Keeta—slapping dresses on hangers against one another in search of just the right one from the dozens of racks around them. My sister, Judy, sits on a hardback chair facing away from me.

The fellow in the chair in front of me lights a cigarette as his wife emerges from the dressing room to ask what he thinks about the new dress she's wearing. He tells her, "Honey, it looks great on you." Of course, I don't comment, but it doesn't.

After the expected long delay, Zola emerges from her dressing room wearing a knee-length, cheerful, coral-colored frock; it is both modest and sharp. She wears it well, since this is "her color." Whether she buys it or not is a question for her alone; she accepts comments, but it's always her decision. Even after years of observing the action, I have no clue what she will do.

....

Zola taught typing and stenography at Plant City High School for almost 20 years, retiring in the early 1960s. She was in every sense a career woman and dressed sedately as a teacher. Upon her retirement, her attire got snappier.

Mom Foster learning to master the Dictaphone at Plant City High School (1952)

Cadillac Yarns

Our troupe of well-dressed shoppers arrived at Maas Brothers soon after it opened on a warm Saturday morning; the damp wind blowing in the car helped make the ride from Plant City comfortable, but I was really looking forward to the air conditioning at the department store. The 25-mile drive to Tampa on Florida State Highway 60 was through a particularly rural stretch of east Hillsborough County. Mom Foster drove her husband's new Cadillac. Pampa bought a new Caddie every year, even though my father sold Lincolns in the same small town.

Keeta sat in the front passenger seat, and Aletha was on the "hump" in the back seat, successfully separating me and Judy. We took this drive with the change of seasons in central Florida—summer, late summer, early fall, almost winter, spring, and early summer—so the females in my family could go dress shopping for the newest fashions. We were accomplished players, and our home stage was Maas Brothers. Leaving Plant City, we passed pastureland around Turkey Creek, strawberry fields at Sydney/Dover, and the Valrico neighborhood. Driving by Valrico prompted Mom Foster to tell her frog story.

Around 1950, she and Pampa lived in Valrico, about 12 miles southwest of Plant City, before buying their home on State Road 39 on the south side of Plant City. Their Valrico home was in a country setting. Mom Foster recalled there was a pond within a few hundred feet of their farmhouse. "It had been a very wet spring, and the pond was full. There were flying bugs and crawling insects everywhere. Now, we had always had frogs around the pond, but that year, their breeding season was intense. Each night, the croaks and calls got louder and went on longer. It was 3 a.m., and Pampa had had enough.

"He got up, put on his pants and shoes, went to the pond, and yelled at the frogs. He had brought a flashlight and that evidently really stirred them up; their calls were deafening. I heard Roy come back into the house and quickly leave again. As the frogs continued their racket, I heard a gunshot, then another. I went to the window that overlooked the pond and saw Roy holding the flashlight in his mouth, shooting and reloading his shotgun as fast as he could as he shot at the pond and its infestation of frogs. This had absolutely no effect on the frogs. He eventually ran out of ammunition and returned to the house looking forlorn. I did manage to get him to laugh about it the next morning."

I had heard the story before, but loved hearing her tell it again; she was a marvelous story teller. The entire cast laughed nonstop as we drove through Brandon.

I told my Valrico story next. I said, "One of my first memories is of turkeys." Mom Foster agreed, "Yes we did try raising turkeys at Valrico." I continued, "Well, Pampa had taken me with him when I was not yet three to help feed the turkeys. It seemed like there were hundreds of them; they were all taller than me, and they looked angry." Mom Foster interjected, "We had about a dozen turkeys, Jim, and they were very large birds." I continued, "Yes, they were. Pampa had tried to get me to help him spread some feed for the monsters, but I refused. He finished feeding them the bag and went to get some more. He told me to wait where I was and said, 'I'll be back in a moment.' Then he was gone.

"The hungry and aggressive bird-beasts encircled me and moved forward. I screamed very loud. Pampa ran back and scattered the turkey beasts. That was my first experience with terror. Pampa comforted me, but it would take me some time to get over that turkey incident." Again, our cast of shoppers cracked up with giggles and chortles, filling the Cadillac. I, of course, laughed along as I always did when I thought I was being funny and made someone laugh.

Keeta said she, too, had a Valrico story. Speaking to Mom Foster, she said, "You and "Dady" (that is the spelling of "Daddy" that my mother and grandmother used in writing about Roy) were living in Valrico and had a couple of horses. You invited L.K. and me to come out to ride. L.K. assured us he was an experienced rider but in fact had almost no experience with horses, particularly high-strung horses like Dady kept. The two of us set out on a short ride and had only gone perhaps a half mile when L.K. said he wanted to go back. Still thinking he knew his horsemanship, I challenged him to a race. I had no sooner kicked my horse to start than his horse reared, throwing him to the ground immediately.

"I stopped and went back to him, and he asked me to help him up. I dismounted and managed to pull him to his feet. His pants were ripped in the back, and he was covered in mud and grass. I couldn't help a slight chuckle. He smiled too, but I could see he was a bit dazed. We made our way back to the barn with my horse in tow, and I got him to the house. He seemed to recover quickly, because we had no sooner retrieved his horse than he decided it was time to go home. We laughed about it later, when he admitted the last time he was on a horse was at age seven."

Over time I noticed that when funny stories about the family were being shared, a male was most frequently the brunt of the humor. This morning's drive was consistent with that observation, and the Cadillac filled with more laughter as we passed the Port of Tampa. As we drove past, we saw a banana boat unloading its conveyor belts full of banana bunches with their pale green hands and fingers. We turned onto Lafayette Street and again on Franklin, parked the car under the Pepsi bottle cap sign, and walked to Maas Brothers.

Scene Two

Aletha was next in the dressing room. Like Zola, she was a size 8 and easy to fit. She and her sister shared very similar tastes in fashion and often wore each other's dresses. She was very slow in choosing a possible purchase, but extremely fast in trying it on and deciding to buy it; it took little encouragement from her family/audience.

The sisters Aletha Beaman (L) and Zola Foster

Aletha E. Beaman was eight years younger than Zola. She owned and operated Bea's Cuddle Shop in Chicago for 22 years before retiring to live with my grandparents in Plant City. She was a successful retail business owner in the 1940s and 1950s. A flashily dressed businesswoman, purple was her favorite color.

After a few years of attending the bimonthly shopping road show to watch my family's women try on shoes or dresses, I had learned to restrict my comments to either silence or emphatic approval. I found the same technique worked best when spending long stretches of time at my other grandmother Zula's dress shop and being asked by one of her customers my opinion of a dress she had tried on.

The waiting and watching reminded me very much of fishing. There were obvious differences, like dressing up for shopping with the ladies and dressing down for fishing. I loved being on the water with Pop. Catching fish was incidental. What mattered was being on an adventure. I also really didn't care whether the women shoppers bought anything or not. It was just a different kind of adventure—a special and social occasion. In both cases, I found laughter and joy with people I loved.

Keeta brought the dress she had just tried on back to the sales clerk, thanked her, and said she would keep looking. She suggested we move on to Junior World on the third floor to find something for Judy. Our cast of five left the Boulevard, and the older man waiting for his wife lit another cigarette.

Walking by the Bridal Salon, I saw one of my favorite acts: a party of seven or eight bridesmaids getting fitted for their dresses. One of the bridesmaids had a toddler in tow. He was the only young child I'd seen on the Floor of Fashion; he was behaving badly but was not as loud or disruptive as several of the young women in the bridal party.

We walked by the bank of elevators and decided to take one up to the next floor. The young lady attendant in white gloves opened the ornate brass doors and took us on our way. In Junior World, Judy made her usual quick selection. Zola asked, "Why don't you try it on?" Judy made the first purchase of the day—a pale blue Carlyle Junior floral print dress featuring a pleated skirt. All agreed it was perfect for school. I expressed no opinion.

Closing Scene

The set for our next scene was the Career Center, back on the second floor. Keeta needed new dresses for the upcoming school year. She had been in the classroom for several years following a change of professional plans to become a chemist, caused by World War II and the births of Judy and me.

Keeta liked modestly cut dresses. She said "Okay" several times to the recurring suggestion of trying one on. She left with two early fall garments—a flower-embroidered charcoal gray wool dress by Jerry Gilden and a dress and coat set in gray wool with black piping by Jane Darby.

Keeta as a fashionable young lady at age 22

Noon approached, and our cast discussed plans for lunch. I
 had a chance to vote, so I suggested the Suncoast
Fountainette on the main floor. The ladies wanted to try
the Colonial Tea Room, but we could see the line of
shoppers waiting for a table was impossibly long. We took
the escalator with spring-coiled handrails down to the
main floor. (Those handrails were unique. You could move
the rings with your fingers as your hand slid up and down
the rail.)

Arriving at the Fountainette, we were led to a table inside
(it was too hot to sit out on the patio) and settled in for
lunch. I knew exactly what I wanted and thoroughly
enjoyed my pimento cheese sandwich with iced tea and
cherry cobbler.

It had been a very good day with the women I loved so
much—yes, Judy too. I looked forward to our next
performance. The ladies agreed over dessert that the next
shopping trip would be for shoes. That was a harder gig for
me.

Still, I knew it would be only a couple of months before it
all began again, with "Why don't you try it on?"

Fishin'

Ahapopka (Muskogee for "trout eating place")

....

We are fishing the shallow-bottomed Lake Apopka, 15 miles northwest of Orlando and 80 miles from Plant City. We begin our time on the water by cruising from the boat launch to a preferred stand of bald cypress. Once we reach our spot, Pop tells me, "Jim, when I was in high school, we fished Lake Apopka. It was bigger and clearer then." He explains, "As part of the war effort, a levee was constructed along the north marshlands and the lake; the levee drained thousands of acres of the lake for farming."

He says that before the draining, the lake had been the second largest lake in the state. He says muck was beginning to form on the lake bottom and the bass population was decreasing annually. "About ten of the fish camps around the lake have closed in the last few years. The seaweed that used to dominate the lake is disappearing, and the bottom is becoming muddy." Pop attributed the damage to the lake to the high levels of phosphate in the fertilizer used in the muck farming in the reclaimed land along the lake.

Me, ready to fish at an early age

We reach the stand of bald cypress a little before sunup—around 6:30. It only takes ten minutes for the Mercury outboard to propel our three-seat, 12-foot aluminum jon boat from the fishing camp to this spot. We start by paddling the boat to a large cypress and tying it off. We both slip over the side of the boat.

We are wading with our cane pole slingshots in three feet of water about 30 feet from the shore in a thicket of cypress trees. The bottom is sandy and firm. We are catching fish regularly. The cypress trees around us are majestic, but as I admire them, I see a four-foot gator ease into the water from a log it had been sunning itself on no more than 30 yards from our spot. Pop and I scramble back into the jon boat.

We usually fish under the shade of a bald cypress, a member of the redwood family. It is a deciduous conifer, but not an evergreen. To reproduce, it produces cones from a single plant's male and female flowers. The mature trees average 40–50 feet high but can reach 100 feet. Some of the taller, slow-growing trees around Lake Apopka are ancient—well over 500 years old.

As the temperature drops in colder months, they lose their feathery pale green spring/summer foliage (with a crown spread upwards of 30 feet), which provides much appreciated shade to me and Pop in the Florida heat. In winter, as the foliage turns reddish, the leaves fall.

The lower trunk, often around six feet in diameter, is buttressed. On the more mature trees, the bark—reddish gray with ridges—has peeled off in long strips. Bald cypress growing in water generates knobby knees around four feet high. Uncertainty surrounds the function of the knees, but they likely aid in respiration and provide structural support. In the 1950s, the knees were used in craftwork such as tables and lamps, but cutting cypress knees was subsequently prohibited under wetlands laws.

Today we fish Lake Apopka for bluegill, a pan fish, and largemouth bass (*Micropterus salmoides*), a sport fish. We begin by targeting bluegill or bream, a member of the sunfish family. They hide near tree stumps or, in our case, cypress knees.

Bream can be found in deep or shallow water, often moving between depths, depending on the time of day. Bluegills also find shelter among water plants and the shade of trees; Lake Apopka has both. They can grow to up to ten inches and three pounds. They prefer small aquatic insects and play a significant role in the food chain as prey for bass, wading birds, and turtles. They are omnivores, eating anything they can fit in their mouths, including foam spiders.

I hold the size 10, single-barb hook between my right thumb and index finger. I pull the fly and the pole-length line tight. The ten-foot bamboo cane pole bends to a 45-degree angle. I release my hold on the barb and the black foam spider fly is slingshot next to a cypress knee. It lands quietly on the lake's surface and initially floats low on the surface—much like an old, dying arthropod might. It then begins to sink very slowly; we're on top of bluegill, and they're having their breakfast. Suddenly, the water breaks with a glimmer of tangerine—a bream flashes her belly as she breaks water, upside down. She turns and rolls on the water's surface, showing olive-colored bands down her side; she vigorously shakes her lavender face and gill cover, trying to dislodge my foam spider.

I let her savor the spider for a second and set the hook with a quick flick of my wrist as she submerges—but not too roughly for fear I'll rip the barb out of her mouth. She swims for the bottom as I raise the pole to bring her back to the surface. She struggles intensely for a few seconds as I lift the pole higher and bring her alongside the boat while she is still submerged. I have ruined her spider breakfast, but she won't be anyone's dinner; she's less than four inches—undersized—although there are technically no size limits in Florida for such pan fish.

Boating her, I carefully remove the hook so that she can continue her breakfast and grow up to be a proper lady. I show her to Pop in the stern of the boat and ease her back into the lake. Pop gets a bite and lands a keeper at over a pound; I cheer him on. We add Pop's fish to the ice chest, which already holds about a dozen bluegill.

We have been up for about five hours, so we decide to eat. I have had a couple of Cokes, water, and a few saltines, and Pop has been drinking coffee from his thermos and water from our canteen. We anchor the boat, and Pop breaks out a tin of sardines and two cans of Vienna sausages, which we split and consume quickly. The main course is peanut butter and guava jelly sandwiches—two each—which we savor while leisurely admiring our surroundings and keeping an eye out for the gator.

The morning is getting warmer, and we decide we need some wind to cool us off. We put our cane polls down in the jon boat and begin preparing our trolling rods and reels; we are going in search of largemouth bass.

....

Bass

Pop and I were freshwater fishermen. We lived within a couple of hours of the Gulf of Mexico, but Pop much preferred the ease, beauty, and safety of fishing the lakes, phosphate pits, and streams of Central Florida, particularly for largemouth bass.

The biggest largemouth bass he ever caught was taken in Fisheating Creek, which is a major natural source of water for Lake Okeechobee. It runs about 45 miles from Highlands County south to Florida's largest lake, Okeechobee, the second largest natural freshwater lake contained entirely in the lower United States. Once, he and his fishing buddies traversed the creek in a 14-foot jon boat fighting bugs, avoiding snakes, and dragging the small boat over stumps and shallow water during their 14-hour journey; they also spotted six gators on the adventure. I was too young to make that trip and never regretted it. Pop's Fisheating Creek trip sounded very hard and unpleasant—except for the bass. The ten-pound beauty resided at the Plant City Ice House for a couple of years before being mounted. Pop caught it on a weedless Johnson Spoon with a green Uncle Josh pork frog trailing behind.

Pop and his trophy bass

Achinaho (Seminole/Creek for "cypress tree")

We fished two lake chains regularly—the Harris Chain (including Lake Apopka) and lakes in and around the Kissimmee Waterway Chain, including Lakes Marion, Pierce, and Hatchineha, the last being our favorite for bass. Lake Hatchineha always delivered fish, at least for us.

We bought a cabin cruiser so Mama and Judy could join us when it didn't interfere with their first love, shopping for dresses. We had success at fishing both at anchor and drifting when we owned the cabin cruiser.

The new boat wasn't designed to catch bass, but we managed just fine. We'd launch from Camp Mack's on the Kissimmee River outside of Lake Wales, where we'd check out the fishing reports and news from other fishermen and load up with live worms and crickets to use as bait for speckled perch and shellcrackers.

Me at the helm of our cabin cruiser (1956)

After a few years, we used the cabin cruiser less frequently. It was considerably more work to maintain and harder to pull and launch. Mama and Judy turned their focus on shopping rather than fishing. Pop sold it and bought another jon boat; there were no tears over the decision.

....

Now it's just me and Pop. We prefer casting to catch bass. Using a Shakespeare casting reel and my Ugly Stick rod feels natural, and I am accurate enough. Our razor-sharp Rapala multibarb hook lure dramatically improves our odds for success.

We are working our way around Lake Hatchineha, about 20 yards offshore. Pop is paddling from the stern, and I'm helping him in the bow. We move the boat around our clockwise journey along the southern shore, edging our way to Catfish Creek. We paddle a few dozen yards in approximately ten-minute increments, unless we get a bite, in which case we linger to induce another bite.

The water is about four feet deep and pretty clear. Our course is set by watching the occasional largemouth break water to swallow a bug or small fish; that helps put us in the right spot—but not too close, for fear of spooking them. We also stay seated, since we've found that standing may give the bass a profile on the surface they wish to avoid.

We avoid making too much noise by moving in the boat or talking; we're not as worried about the largemouth hearing us as we are about maintaining the serenity of the moment as we cast and reel in. Yes, we can hear distant buzzing outboards, but we also hear the call of birds, the screech of raptors, the hum of insects, and water lapping against the side of the boat.

The setting is spectacular, with the red-cast bald cypress mixed with graying Spanish moss. Under a nearby tall cypress, two white great egrets are fishing up to their knees, using their dagger beaks at the end of their long, s-curved necks to spear the occasional perch. Behind the two wading birds, a third is standing on the shore, its wings spread to a full 50 inches.

A largemouth breaks the water near us. We both cast a few feet from where she's feeding; I'm on her near side, and Pop casts over her—under the overhang of a large clump of moss a few feet above the water's surface. We let the bass's hunger and inbred, territorial claim move it to the Rapala. With a slow and deliberate reel-in, the lure is irresistible to a hungry largemouth.

She goes for Pop's lure, and he hooks her cleanly. I pull in my line and sit back to watch the struggle; it continues for two or three minutes. The bass jumps clear of the water once and breaks the surface with a roll twice. She pulls the boat around a few feet as she tries to flee. The line and pole are bent almost double as she dives, and the brake on the reel begins to slip. She wears herself out as I grab the fishing net and swoop her up.

She's about two-and-a-half pounds and a beauty: greenish brown with a faded belly. Her exaggerated mouth extends from beyond the rear of the jaw, and she has caught the Rapala in her lip by the hooks at the end of the lure. Even on the deck of the boat, she's still protesting, although with increasingly less anger, as if she's resigned to her destiny. Pop carefully and quickly removes the hook and places her in the ice chest. As she lands in the ice, she slaps her tail on it a couple of times, to say goodbye to the lake. The noises from the chest cease within a couple of minutes. She was a worthy combatant and a gorgeous treasure.

....

It should be universally accepted that anglers lie. They exaggerate the weight and length of the fish they've caught—even the species of fish. They will tell you about fish that got away that never existed, and stories about the battles fought to land a mighty fish extend well into the absurd. Such lies are harmless and add romance to the sport. My fishing lies were the only fibs of mine that Pop and I could both laugh about.

Scout Camp

Troop 5

I was a second generation Troop 5 Boy Scout. My Pop was a Scout in the early 1930s. Pop loved camping and was directly involved in my learning to love it as well.

We weren't the only father and son with that connection. My friend Doug's dad became the first Troop 5 boy to become an Eagle Scout and was a Scout with Pop. Troop 5 was founded in 1931 and had a rich history. In fact, in 1933, the entire troop of 35 Scouts achieved Eagle Scout status.

Plant City Troop Made Up Entirely of Eagle Boy Scouts

1933 —Photo by Lovett, Plant City.

Troop No. 5, Boy Scouts, of Plant City, became an Eagle Scout troop with the advancing of 13 boys to Eagle Scout on Monday night. They are, left to right, front row: Scoutmaster O. E. Baynard, Aaron Wheeler, Dan Clark, Robert White, Maring Clark, George Garrett, Paul Lanier, Frank Schulte, Billy Taylor, Alex Sanchez, Assistant Scoutmaster Mike E. Sansone. Second row: Roy Hurst, Douglass Harwell, Earl Crawford, Madison Kilgore, Craig Mills, Joe Martin, E. J. DeVane, John Park, Bill Floyd, Bernice Davis. Third row: Whit Marvin, DeWitt Carlton, George Higgins, Jack Duncan, Sid Johnson, Heyward Davis, Marvin Abbott, Kenneth Cason, Jason Scarborough, David Carlton. Fourth row: Edwin Harwell, S. Lenny Cason, Asa R. Lorrick, Bob Mack, Victor Smith, T. B. Mack.
The troop is sponsored by the Norman McLeod post of the American Legion.

....

Doug starts crowing at exactly 6:15 a.m., just after first light. I don't understand how it is possible to be so precise; he has no watch. He crows three times, just as he was instructed the night before, and he sounds very much like a rooster. I am sleeping soundly near Doug's hammock. His cock-a-doodle-dos wake me and all the other Scouts at our camp. I hit my head on the fabric roof of my jungle hammock—I am suddenly (but not surprisingly) awake. Having seen Mr. Panos do similar "entertainments" successfully, I had every confidence the hypnosis would work.

I unzip my hammock, spread back the mosquito netting, and roll out onto the ground. I see Doug with his hands folded under his armpits, flapping his elbows—most chicken-like. I start laughing, and the other boys join in. Mr. Panos walks up to Doug and claps his hands twice; the flapping stops immediately.

Doug looks confused, but seeing the rest of the troop laughing, he grins broadly and begins laughing, too. The post-hypnotic suggestion Mr. Panos planted the night before around the campfire has worked as promised.

Yesterday, the morning started at our Scout building next to Norman McLeod American Legion Post #26 (our sponsoring organization) in west Plant City. We hiked six miles to Scout Forest, Coronet Lake, and our piney campsite. We had a swim in the lake, and Bobby, Doug, Ken, and I qualified for our swimming merit badges. The requirements included diving, floating, and swimming a series of strokes—sidestroke, backstroke, and front crawl—for 150 yards.

Troop 5 Court of Honor, late 1950s (me, fourth from right)

Our campsite is within a few yards of the lake and about a quarter mile from the Coronet Industries phosphate processing plant. The forest we are in consists of thousands of mature pine trees planted in neat rows and columns and a full carpet of ground cover—mostly saw palmetto plants (*Serenoa*), some reaching seven feet. We always enjoy Coronet Lake, but it isn't much of a challenge, given its proximity to our homes, the ease of access, and its rather settled nature.

Withlacoochee (Muskhogean for "little big water")

We hike through the Croom Tract of Withlacoochee State Forest three miles upstream to a launch site on the Withlacoochee. The 140-mile river flows north in this stretch between Hernando and Sumter Counties as it makes its way to the Gulf of Mexico. The canoes are waiting for us in Mr. Keller's truck, about 50 yards away. There is lots of chatter and laughter as we enter the river. The river water is refreshingly cool, and although you can see the sand bottom, it is tannin-stained.

We will be on the river for about three hours as we wend our way to our campsite. The river is about six feet deep and ranges from 30 to 60 feet wide, meandering every few hundred feet; we go northwest, due north, northeast, due east, northwest, and due west on our journey. The banks are wooded, and when the river narrows, the crowns of the moss-covered cypress trees and oaks on both sides of the river touch, providing a canopy of shade.

Almost every big turn in the river exposes a deserted white, sandy beach. There are two back-to-back oxbow (180-degree) turns with a broad beach on the neck of the second. We put in our canoes and, as Mr. Panos predicted, find a rich bed of paper pondshell mussels (*Utterbackia imbecillis*).

They are about three inches long, with thin greenish-yellow, oblong, semi-edible shells. We dig out about a dozen each from the submerged sand along the shore and store them in the canoes. On our last leg of the trip, we are surrounded by pond cypress trees, which themselves are surrounded by knees, slash pine, hickory, and various oaks. We see wood storks, swallow-tailed kites, a bald eagle, and several hawks along the way.

We put ashore at the beach near the campsite. We discard a few dead mussels from our stock—mussels can live several days out of the water, and if we have a dead one, there is no telling how long ago it died. We immediately place the mussels in several buckets of clean water from the pump so they will purge themselves of sand and grit. They spend their whole lives beneath the sand, constantly filtering sand and grit—purging is what they do best.

We have another swim in the lake, and some of the Scouts do a little fishing, again with success. The mussels have soaked for over three hours, long enough to have purged themselves of their sand. We scrape their shells, first with the back of a knife and then with a wire brush, to remove debris and sand, then drain the buckets and submerge them in fresh water. Some of the mussels have "beards"— sticky membranes used to attach themselves to stable surfaces.

Satisfied with our preparations, we begin fire-roasting the 70 mussels. We place them in improvised aluminum foil roasting pans, adding olive oil, garlic cloves, and parsley, and we've browned some crusty bread to sop up the juices.

No one eats more than two. The mussels crunch, like the sound of ground glass when it's stepped on. The grit and sand are overwhelming. It is our troop's first complete fail at cooking for ourselves. Several of us swear off mussels for good.

Luckily, the fishing that afternoon went quite well, and we have plenty of spare provisions. We recover quickly after supper and have a fun night around the campfire. Mr. Panos and two of the fathers who have joined us tell ghost stories until late. We sing and laugh. We've had a good day.

Jamboree

I leave Tampa's Union Station at 12:01 p.m. on Saturday, July 16, 1960, aboard Atlantic Coast Line #92 outbound for Jacksonville. I will celebrate my 13th birthday in Colorado Springs among 56,000 other boys attending the Golden Jubilee National Jamboree of the Boy Scouts of America. I've been assured that it will be a wonderful experience. After leaving Tampa, we begin lunch in the dining car just as we go through Plant City. Passing through Jacksonville, the lights are turned down and I try to fall asleep in the coach car, without success. I can't really stretch out flat, and I'm frustrated.

Along with a couple other Boy Scouts, I climb into the empty baggage bin above my head with my train-issued pillow and fall into a deep slumber without delay. For the rest of my trip, I use this technique to sleep at night, and by the end of the trip, the baggage racks are full of slumbering Scouts.

Monday morning, we arrive in Kansas City. We enter the Central Great Plains before dark. The emptiness of the land is staggering, the horizon boundless. The next day we pull into Pueblo, Colorado. We have climbed almost 4,000 feet since leaving Kansas City, but the ascent is so gradual it's hard to detect. We depart Pueblo on the Denver & Rio Grande Western Railroad, arriving in Colorado Springs later that morning. We take buses to the Jamboree site, eight miles north of Colorado Springs, and begin setting up camp.

We have traveled about 1,800 miles since leaving Tampa. I enjoyed the time on the train more than the stops. The rhythm of a train is comforting: the measured rocking of the car, the sound of the wheels on the track, and the regular schedule of meals and "lights out." Watching the landscape change dramatically over a couple of hours is beguiling. There is a sudden rush when a train going in the other direction passes by. The train horn becomes a comfort and never disturbs me in my sleeping perch.

The 1960 Golden Jubilee National Jamboree marks the 50th anniversary of the Boy Scouts of America. It is only the fifth such National Jamboree in Scout history. Scouts from 38 countries are represented. The theme of the Jamboree is "For God and Country."

Our mess tent and camp kitchen at the Jamboree

The Jamboree opens on Friday at the main stage, with 200 Native Americans depicting Indian life in a large tepee village. Actor James Arness (Marshall Matt Dillon of *Gunsmoke*) narrates a story of the old west. There are fireworks that night off nearby Pikes Peak that go on for an hour.

On Sunday, my birthday, a somewhat united Protestant worship service is held, with over 30,000 Scouts marching into the natural amphitheater and taking seats in an orderly fashion. It is hot and cloudless, which I'm used to, but the 20 mph wind is dry and scorching, unlike Florida's moist breezes. Lots of boys are carried off with heat exhaustion, and some end up in the hospital. I have enough sense to keep my cap on throughout the morning. Our counselor instructed us to bring canteens of water; I sip often and lightly.

I am ready to leave after 20 minutes of a two-hour service. I am ready to leave Colorado Springs as well, as we trudge our way back to camp.

I'm not particularly homesick. I am tiring of the "manfulness" of the event in Colorado. Although I haven't yet reached sexual maturity, girls occupy my thoughts, and I am skilled at flirting with them. I enjoy their company somewhat more than that of boys.

We depart Colorado on Friday in the mid-afternoon aboard the Colorado-Southern Railway special train outbound for Dallas, New Orleans, and Tampa. We eat all our meals on the train, and seeing the countryside slide by engages me again.

We arrive in New Orleans around 7 a.m. on Sunday. We have lunch and tour the French Quarter, then depart New Orleans that evening on the Louisville & National special train to Tampa. This railway is the tenth we've taken on our 3,000 mile adventure. I am ready to be home.

Me detraining in Tampa

....

I took the Boy Scouts seriously for about three years (and the camping for longer), reaching Star Scout level, but I lost my ambition to become an Eagle Scout. The regimentation that Scouts practice didn't particularly bother me. I was a good Scout, carried my weight, was an amiable teammate, and tried to live up to the Scout oath and law—but the law ends with being reverent, and that's not one of my strengths..

Mostly, scouting was a fun time with good friends and my Pop, sharing the joy of being outside in nature.

Tomlin — Startin' In

Seventh

Mary L. Tomlin was born around 1876. She was the first principal of the school named for her in the 1930s, Tomlin Junior High School. My sister went to Tomlin in 1955 and 1956 and would complete her student teaching there in the mid-1960s. I attended Tomlin from 1959 to 1961. The principal was James W. Jordan. It was a good place for me, and if his leadership was responsible for that, I thank him.

I began seventh grade scholastically successful. I was taking advanced classes and doing well. I was recognized for my grasp of English, and I liked to read—but only books that interested me. Furthermore, I did well in math and science. However, I drifted academically as the year progressed. I started with an overall B average, including a B in conduct. By the start of the new year, my grades dipped to a C average, and my conduct scores, although never rock-bottom, ebbed. But my personal happiness crested. I was a happy, above-average boy who enjoyed his classmates and friendships.

I was back with friends from kindergarten I had lost touch with due to attending different grade schools. This was very comforting, and my old friendships rekindled quickly. I was also making friends with classmates I didn't know before. I walked to my grandmother Helms' house every day for a glorious lunch and went downtown after school almost every day. It was an especially fun time.

Me in junior high school

I had several social hubs: there was school itself and nearby Courier Field Park for sports; Central Pharmacy for fountain drinks, hanging out with pals, and mingling with the opposite sex; the Hi-Fi House for pinball; and the Hillsborough County courthouse for a different kind of show. Each location had its own feel and tone. All of the players and crowds in those settings engaged me more than the academic program at Tomlin.

Beatniks

I didn't know Ralph until junior high school. He was always in a good mood and was popular with the entire class. He was six feet tall, and his personality gave him additional height. We met thanks to my selling him pieces of homemade cornbread I would bring back to school after lunch at my grandmother's house. He was a reliable customer. We'd spend a few minutes at the school auditorium's west entrance before the bell rang, enjoying our hoecakes. That often led to a fight.

We began "beatnik fighting" for our own pleasure. Neither of us was "bohemian," but we both thought Maynard G. Krebs on the TV show *The Many Loves of Dobie Gillis* was the best character. As the stereotypical beatnik, he was amiable and pseudointellectual—as were our weekly fights. Unlike my elementary school fights, these were good-natured and fun.

The object of the "fight" was to make the other person laugh or lose composure. As long as there was no physical contact, we could subject each other to placement in awkward positions and use taunts, props, and distractions. We alternated as antagonist and target. We would go three rounds. The winner of a round was declared when the target laughed or broke his required silence or stoic deportment. One of my "attacks" on Ralph was sneaking a bottle of Wonder soap bubbles in my pocket and blowing bubbles in his face. He almost hurt himself laughing so hard. He graciously raised my arm over our heads to show his submission. We drew a crowd.

The following week, Ralph had me tussle my own bushy hair. He then pulled several clothes pins from his pocket and had me stick them in my hair. The audience had grown as a result of reviews from our earlier match. The crowd loved it when I declared Ralph the winner.

I did impressions like Red Skelton's Gertrude the Seagull or Jonathan Winters' Maude Frickert. Ralph told silly or slightly risqué jokes that equaled or surpassed my impressions. We made faces, contorted our bodies into silly positions, played armpit fart melodies, and did silly dance steps to make each other laugh. We allowed props, so we often brought a paper bag with items such as a lady's hat, fake mustache, clown nose, and once, a Halloween mask of a dog, which was accompanied by lots of barking and leg raising. We were evenly matched and often fought to a draw. We were our best audience, but by the end of the school year, we had become a bit of a hit.

Band

I joined the Tomlin band and originally picked the clarinet as my instrument. Judy played flute at Plant City High School and had just taken first chair. She practiced hard and was naturally talented; I did not and was not. My natural instrument was my voice, but I really liked band, and the other guys and gals were fun. I decided to be cool and go big with the baritone saxophone. The case was 48 inches long and, with the sax inside, weighed about 18 pounds. It made a fine bludgeon.

The other baritone sax player in the Tomlin band was Robbie. He and I were in Boy Scouts together, and we played on the same Little League team—we were close buddies. Robbie was a big boy, and I was tall, and we were both well coordinated. After a few days of carrying our baritone saxes back and forth to band practice, we found if we held the case with both hands and started spinning in a circle, we could hold the load with one arm as we picked up speed. We tested our spinning exercise and soon discovered that if Robbie spun in one direction and I in the other, then brought the two cases together, all kinds of pandemonium followed.

The two cases colliding made a loud crashing sound, and a shockwave went through us that made our arms tingle. We never struck each other. The weight of the sax-bludgeon we suddenly felt in our single arm (along with being a bit dizzy) made us lose our balance, and one or both of us ended up on the ground. It was major fun. We were never hurt, and the instruments and cases suffered no significant damage. I was much better at swinging the sax than playing it.

One day, as we had a spinning sax battle, we had both just fallen and a woman driving by saw the aftermath. She stopped, got out of her car, walked up to us, and asked if we were okay. We were dizzy and couldn't stand up yet, but we started laughing. She joined in without us ever answering her. Then she got back in her car, waved, and drove off.

Robbie and I would talk about our sax fights some time later. He swore we fought with clarinets. I believed it was saxes. Saxes makes a better story.

Drugstores

Herring's Pharmacy in the 1940s

Drugstores are an integral part of our family's history. My father met my mother in 1939 outside of Herring's Pharmacy in Plant City. He had aspirations of becoming a pharmacist and was working there. She was a college student taking a year off and wanted to be a chemist. Mary Tillman introduced Pop to her, and he engaged in some fine flirting. Pop would tell anyone who listened that upon seeing her, he fell in love and after my mother left the drugstore, told a co-worker, "I will marry that woman someday." My mother relished his recollection. She also knew Pop flirted—with waitresses, sales clerks, and the women in their bridge club. She accepted it, because she knew he wouldn't go too far and because that was who he was when they first met. They flirted with each other for their entire 50-year marriage. They even developed a private whistle they used if they were separated in a crowd or wanted to find each other. The entire family adopted the whistle:

My family's private whistle

In junior high, I spent many hours at White's Central Pharmacy run by W. B. Herring's nephews, Jack and Dick White. It was a short walk downtown from Tomlin to the southeast corner of Reynolds Street and Collins. One of the White brothers was almost always on site, keeping an eye on the teenagers who flocked to the drugstore after school for a cherry smash or lemon or vanilla Coke; included with the drink was a small pretzel hung on the straw. There were three booths wide enough for four kids on each side. We would get to Central Pharmacy before high school let out and have the run of the place for about an hour. Once the older teenagers showed up, we tended to break up and start for home or find other entertainments.

White's Central Pharmacy

Flirting

I took every opportunity to flirt with girls. Along with the two movie theaters in town (the Capitol and State), Central Pharmacy was a prime location for that. Normally, the girls sat separately from the boys. There were no rules about segregating the sexes, but that's how it always started out. I was quick to reject the premise, because I've always had a genuine interest in the female perspective. After a few minutes of talking with the guys, I would work my way to the girls' table, stand, and listen closely to their conversation. Picking my moment and my words carefully, I would comment on their conversation. I got good at it with practice. I invariably asked politely if I could sit down with the girls and never got a "no." I really tried to make them feel comfortable and laugh. I was usually successful.

I flirted all day long at school by making eye contact and talking to girls I found engaging. Physical beauty, although helpful, was not essential, but good humor and sound intellect were. I flirted in class when I should have been studying, during tests, in the halls going to class, and in the schoolyard. I was largely there to flirt.

Flirting is an exchange, but it's more of a roundabout than an intersection; it should flow, not start and stop. It is a process rather than a system. Flirting is a learnable skill, but some baseline abilities are helpful: a quick wit, an easy smile and laugh, an ability to kid as well as take ribbing, and compassion shown by listening and focusing on the other person and her reactions—and, oh yes, sometimes, when you are really happy and in the moment, your eyes twinkling.

Accomplished flirting is nuanced, self-effacing, attentive, open, and spontaneous. Think of a comment or response quickly; don't sound it out it in your mind, just take a fast taste of the word or phrase and learn to trust your inner voice. Use of the absurd is effective, and being quick with a sincere apology is important if the flirter touches a nerve. Watching those observing the flirtation also helps you gain helpful feedback. Having a strong vocabulary and being well read are beneficial. Interrupting the other person breaks the flow and natural feeling of flirtation. Touching may ensue, but in junior high school, that wasn't the point.

Flirting is part of human nature—it can lead to procreation of the species, a good thing. Flirting doesn't have to have a sexual payoff, though—I flirted with my pets, both cats and dogs. People are always flirting with babies and for the camera.

My two grandmothers flirting with Judy and the camera

Tomlin – Goin' Out

Eighth

In eighth grade, I ended up with an overall B average, but my grades in science and algebra were borderline. My conduct was a bit below average, but no Ds or Fs. I was never tardy and missed only a total of eight-and-a-half days of school. My academic efforts included sort of paying attention in class, no note taking, and no homework, but a good deal of recreational reading and further development of my social skills; I talked a lot.

Donna

A single event in Plant City would define that year of school; it was played on an international stage. She passed through Plant City around midnight on Saturday, September 10, 1960, with winds approaching 100 mph. Our family had been monitoring the progress of the storm all day following her landfall in the middle Keys earlier that morning as a Category 4 hurricane with sustained winds of 145 mph. Pop had installed a 30-foot TV antenna a few years earlier when he worked at the Westinghouse store. It was able to bring in Tampa television station WTVT, Channel 8, with a fairly clear black and white picture. We had been watching Roy Leep, the station's chief meteorologist, throughout the morning, and his forecasts and updates were becoming more ominous. My parents decided to begin preparations for the storm that had caused so much damage in the Caribbean.

My parents, sister, and I spent the day filling up the bathtub and jugs with water, removing potential missiles like trash cans and bicycles from the yard, and gathering candles. We stocked up on canned meat, chili and beans, peanut butter, crackers, powdered milk, fresh fruit, and bread. We owned several ice chests and filled them with blocks of ice Pop and I got from the ice house on North Palmer Street. We bought kerosene fuel for the Coleman lantern, lighter fluid, and charcoal for the barbeque grill, and a dozen extra batteries for the transistor radios and flashlights. Around 4 p.m., Pop cranked down the TV antenna to its lowest point and I helped him put some cement blocks in the bottom of the boat stored under the carport to anchor it.

It had rained intermittently throughout the day as bands of showers from Donna came through. The wind began picking up around 3 p.m., with gusts in the 20 mph range. The heavy rain began around 7:30 p.m., just as night fell. The weather deteriorated quickly after that. The front porch screen was sliced in one panel to prevent it from blowing away, the lantern was pumped and tested, and the windows in the house were closed with the exception of two left open a crack—one on the east side and the other on the north side—so that a sudden change in air pressure wouldn't damage the house. The power went off, so we lit the lantern and tuned in the transistor radio to follow the storm.

We began checking the attic for leaks, which was a bit daunting, because we were using flashlights and the wind was howling just over our heads. We found several leaks and placed a pot or bucket under each. We heard a tree fall close to our house, but we were confident it hadn't hit us. Although we were tempted to sneak a quick look out the back door, we decided that was not smart. Had it not been for the formidable danger, we would have seen a terrific and horrific show. The sound outside was intense, the house creaked mournfully, and time passed slowly. We ate sandwiches my mother had prepared earlier and entertained ourselves by playing cards around the dining room table and the Coleman lantern.

The turmoil of a hurricane has beauty; although violent and life-threatening, Donna performed an extended dance of the elements. The wind and blowing rain built over a period of hours until her intensity reached the extreme as the center of the storm approached with its furious eye wall. As the eye drifted over, the careening whirl ceased in an eerie stillness, as though Donna needed to catch her breath. The wind then suddenly reversed, and she danced in reverse, but this time it began with the fiercest leaps, turns, and cavorting of the entire show. As she moved off stage, she lingered, as if she was sorry to leave.

The path of hurricane Donna
Attribution: Florida Keys – Public Libraries from Key West, Florida, USA
Creativecommons.org/

By dawn, she was gone and off to the Atlantic and the Mid-Atlantic States for another devastating performance later in the week. The weather in Plant City improved by the hour. The wind dropped below 30 mph, and the rain turned to drizzle. It was hot without the attic fan, and we wanted to go outside, but we knew it wasn't safe. We settled for sitting on our front porch and gaining our footing again; there was laughter. We could see that the tree we heard fall earlier missed everyone's property, but it did take down some power lines. We all decided we needed sleep, since we had only slept for an hour or two the night before. We ate snacks from our well-stocked provisions and retired; I was still excited and found sleep difficult, but eventually I closed the curtain on Donna.

Hi-Fi

A couple of doors down from Central Pharmacy was the Hi-Fi House with a Bally pinball machine. My father had worked for a while at a jukebox company and sold pinball machines in that role, so my family didn't object to my spending time at the Hi-Fi House. Many families took a much harsher view of pinball machines, because that industry was associated with gambling and bad behavior. At the Hi-Fi House, songs were always playing on the loudspeakers, and the manager welcomed teenagers. The back room held a fine pinball machine that entertained me, Ken, Red, Tommy, Dennis, Beaver, Spruce, and Rat. We'd linger at the Hi-Fi House for an hour or two, until the manager tired of us.

We fed the machine our coins, and some of us got very good with the flippers and at pushing the limits of the tilt sensors. The pinball machine was captivating: the sound of the plunger releasing a ball down the shooter lane, the ball rolling around the playfield and bouncing off bumpers, the whirr of the spinners being turned by a ball passing through a gate, the flashing light show from the light box, mechanical sounds from the machine's innards, and the chime when an end-of-game bonus led to a free play.

Some of the town's most interesting people frequented the Hi-Fi House, including Floyd Jolly or, as he preferred, just "Jolly." I understood he had been hurt in a motorcycle accident years before, and, when I knew him, he went about town on a bicycle, always whistling. He was probably in his thirtes, with a full beard and a dime in his ear that he said he kept there so he would never be broke. He painted quarters with red fingernail polish on one side so that he could recognize them once they had been thoroughly circulated through the economy. He enjoyed watching us play pinball and listen to the music that was a constant in the store. He was a gentle, good-natured man—until someone accepted his challenge to thumb wrestle. He was missing half of his middle finger, which often led guys to think he would be a pushover in a thumb wrestling match. I never saw him lose, and he often did some real damage to the other player's finger.

Over the course of a week, I'd hear almost every genre of music: pop, rock and roll, country, classical, gospel, show tunes, jazz, Latin, even opera. The music at the Hi-Fi House was the best I'd ever heard. The manager would play a record upon request, and when he received a shipment of new albums, he'd add to the selection not only the favorites of his customers, but his own. Many afternoons, I spent more time browsing through the albums, reading the liner notes, and listening to song after song than playing pinball. My favorite artists and musical styles were the ones I was unfamiliar with.

Court

Ken and I enjoyed going to the Hillsborough County courthouse to observe misdemeanor and traffic court proceedings. The courthouse on Michigan Avenue was air-conditioned and offered relief from the Florida summer heat, as well as some unique entertainment. The defendants were often sympathetic and, at other times, pathetic. It was all very decorous, except when a frequent suspect resorted to falsehoods, tears, and arguing. The judges were patient and professional, but on rare occasions, their frustration with a particularly difficult defendant registered. The police officers giving testimony were interesting because of their various styles of presenting information to the court. Ken and I noticed that one officer commonly missed his court date—in such cases, the defendant walked, which frustrated the judge. We had our favorite players on both sides of the law and looked forward to seeing them in action.

The courthouse had other delightful characters, too. Regrettably, I never knew his real name, but Blind Charlie was a fine example. He sold peanuts and could be seen at high school football games, around town, and almost every court day at the courthouse. His parched peanuts were superb, and he was a genuinely pleasant fellow. Ken and I would tell him about the interesting cases we had heard that day, and he was always interested in the details—and in us.

Part Five – Adolescent

Cheatin'

Attic Keys

I'm sorry, but it was too easy. It was also wrong, but mostly it was too easy. Climbing 12 steps brought me to the keys—keys of all kinds: algebra, English, and science— all right there. They were stored in our attic in cardboard boxes clearly labeled by grades 1–12. My mother had been doing "homebound" teaching for Hillsborough County Schools for a year or so, visiting disabled students in all grades to keep them on track with their education. Several of her stash of textbook keys matched my class textbooks at Tomlin Junior High.

I limited my use of the keys: I never made the honor roll in junior high school, I didn't copy the answers and take them to tests, and I relied on my memory to recall the correct answers in class. I just wanted to know the answers to textbook questions without making the effort of reading the material or paying close attention in class. I forfeited a good deal in this academic cheating: the pleasure of digging deeply into a subject, understanding the nuances of the subject matter, my integrity, and my self-respect. I suspect I cheated myself at least as much as I cheated my student cohorts, teachers, and the educational system.

When I was in the attic, cheating, I became easily distracted. I found old photograph albums interesting, and two large boxes of old comic books often seduced me to such an extent that I'd forget to cheat. I found books other than those I was assigned that I would examine and often read. I began reviewing the keys for textbooks that were outside my class curriculum; I was learning despite my worst intentions.

I will not minimize the misuse of mother's teaching keys; it was bad, and I regret it.

Snowin'

Josiah Bernard Martin, my 12th grade English teacher, was an accomplished educator who made me think. He had an intellectual edge that was fun and challenging at times but unsettling and off-putting at others. In March 1965, Mr. Martin assigned an essay on friendship. I had a solid grasp of English at that age and was making acceptable grades in his class. Sometimes in class, he and I would engage in light repartee—I would push back politely with whatever wit I could muster when his questions or comments (to me or my classmates) bothered me sufficiently. I believed he at least somewhat enjoyed my good-natured impudence, and I appreciated his willingness to engage with me.

As usual, I had waited until the last minute to begin my paper. Normally, I had no problem cranking out a written assignment or even writing a speech. This "friendship" paper was on one of my favorite subjects, and I wanted it to be well thought out and well constructed, but I had run out of time to accomplish either. I went to the attic, not to find a key (which, of course, didn't exist for an essay), but to find material on friendship that I could use in writing my paper. I found a book of Francis Bacon (1561–1626) essays.

Bacon wrote in his essay *Of Friendship* (1612, rewritten 1625): "A principal fruit of friendship is the ease and discharge of the fullness and swellings of the heart, which passions of all kinds do cause and induce. We know diseases of stoppings and suffocations are the most dangerous in the body; and it is not much otherwise in the mind; you may take sarza to open the liver, steel to open the spleen, flower of sulphur for the lungs, castareum for the brain; but no receipt openeth the heart but a true friend, to whom you may impart griefs, joys, fears, hopes, suspicions, counsels, and whatsoever lieth upon the heart to oppress it, in a kind of civil shrift or confession."

I committed an act of rank plagiarism by paraphrasing Bacon without attribution.

Mr. Martin read my essay and called me into a private conference. He told me he knew I had plagiarized my essay. He said he was determined to track down the original work and author. I denied it. He likely spent some time in his research and, after a week or two, spoke to me again. He told me he couldn't find the source but was confident I had stolen the material. He gave me an F on the paper and for that entire grading term. I didn't contest it.

Mr. Martin and I enjoyed each other's company but never showed that to others or admitted it to each other. I know I liked him, and he wrote in my senior yearbook an obtusely friendly note, with exclamation point.

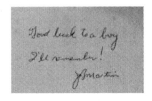

Mr. Martin's note in my yearbook

After I received my F, we never discussed the incident again. We were polite and, at times, friendly. I backed off needling him, and he seemed to go easier on me for the last semester of his class; I received a B for that term. I haven't engaged in such overt plagiarism since. We both knew that I had cheated. However, I never told Mr. Martin that Bacon was my source. That may have aggravated him, but possibly it entertained him as well.

I have avoided mortal sin. But the deadly sin, sloth, has always been a challenge to me unless I feel some passion for a thing. If there is no passion, I float through an experience as quickly and shallowly as possible. My dear friend Mark Dawson wrote a note in my senior yearbook addressing me as "JBM" for Josiah B. Martin, since Mark also argued with Mr. Martin in class.

> *J.B.M. (for Martin)*
> *I also smile when I think of you and all the things you've done. In fact, I laugh! Seriously, you have an amazingly wide read intellect which I respect very much. If you would stop trying to snow everybody all the time you would really be a good kid. Let's go get stoned tonight. I've got the money.*
> *Mark*

Mark's note in my freshman yearbook

Dixie

"Stop!" is all she said, as she blocked the front door to Reynolds Street. My friend, Carl, and I froze. (I always tried to work with an accomplice, because having a partner in crime builds courage and provides someone to share in the excitement.) The waitress was in her forties and petite—a little over five feet tall. She had short red hair, glasses, and an angry blaze in her brown eyes.

She stood with her feet firmly planted and her arms spread open covering the doorway. She slowly extended her right arm, open-handed, palm up. With her left hand, she pointed to her open palm and poked her empty right hand several times. We dug into our pockets and gave her all the change we had, about $1.50 each in coins from quarters to pennies. It was more than we had taken from the empty tables following the Dixie Restaurant lunch rush, but we were not in a position to pursue that loose end.

She said in the sternest of voices, "You are stealing tips from some very hard-working ladies who depend on that money to live. I will make it my business to warn every waitress in Plant City about you two. If I ever see you try something like you just did, I will see to it that the police are called." We both apologized immediately. I told her we wouldn't do it again. She looked us over closely and after a few seconds, moved away from the door so we could leave; we never stole tips again.

As we fetched our bikes from the stand behind the Capital Theater, we didn't speak, which was rare. Carl and I didn't laugh about our transgression afterward, which was extraordinary, but it was too scary to trivialize.

Nabbed

Ken was my next accomplice in petty theft a few months later. It was after school, and we were downtown, finishing our Cokes and flirting with girls at White's Central Pharmacy. I was running low on paper and pencils and told Ken I wanted to pick up some at McCrory's 5 & Dime before going home. We entered the store at the Collins Street entrance and walked to the school supply area—pencils were on one aisle and lined paper on the other side in the adjoining aisle. I asked Ken to get two packs of paper.

I waited until he reached that area and made eye contact. I picked up two 12-packs of pencils and, making sure Ken was watching, raised the back of my untucked shirt, shoved the pencils under my waistband, and lowered my shirt tail again to hide the bounty.

Ken smiled as I walked around the counter and dropped two packs of paper in the back of my pants. We looked around and were satisfied no one had seen me. We made our way to the Evers Street exit, and, as we were approaching the door, two sales clerks—a man and a woman—stopped us by blocking our way. That felt familiar to me. We did our best to act confused and upset, which didn't work at all.

Ken and I were ordered to follow them to the store manager's office, sit down, and wait for the store manager. The woman clerk left to find the manager, and the male clerk glared at us silently. After a lengthy delay, the manager, Otis Andrews, entered the office and told us to stand up. He said, "I know both of you and your families. I think they would want me to teach you a lesson. Place the items you stole on the desk." I did. He picked up the phone next to the pencils and dialed a number.

"Officer, I have two boys here who we caught shoplifting." We couldn't hear the other person on the phone, but Mr. Andrews said, "Yes, I would like to press charges." After the manager hung up, Ken and I began begging him to let us pay for the pencils and paper and to let us go; we had more than enough money on us to do that. He emphatically declined. He stood across from us with his arms crossed and looked quite stern. I was panicked, and Ken looked worse. In the several minutes it took for the police to show up, time became leaden and interminable. Waiting for the cops in the office was the first time my knees trembled.

Two uniformed Plant City police officers came into the office and told us to follow them. I held out some hope that they would take us outside, give us a strong lecture, and let us go, but they looked very displeased. As we left the store by the Collins Street doors, we turned left, walked to Reynolds Street, and saw a parked squad car. I stumbled, and Ken stopped suddenly; things had just gotten serious.

One cop opened the street side door to the back seat of the cruiser and told us to climb in; we silently did as asked. We didn't look at each other as we scrunched down as far as we could. The ride to the station was humiliating and scary. Once we all too slowly traveled the three or four blocks to the police station, we were escorted into the main room and told to stand in front of a large metal desk. Another officer entered and sat at the desk. He told us in the gruffest of voices, "I'm here to book you for theft."

Ken and I finally made eye contact and reflected each other's self-pity and fear brilliantly, I'm sure. We asked if we were going to jail. There was a long pause, dragged out theatrically by the booking officer. He started to speak, stopped, and got up from the desk. He finally replied, "I need to go talk to my sergeant, and let's see what he says." He left us there for at least 20 minutes marinating in the gloom. While he was gone, I wondered if we would have to go to court for our crimes and, if so, how we would explain ourselves to Blind Charlie, our courthouse friend.

Bobby was a Hillsborough County sheriff's deputy and motorcycle cop at the time. He was on duty when over the police radio he heard of two boys being held for shoplifting at the Plant City jail—one being his nephew—ah, that would be me.

Me and Uncle Bobby early on

He later told me his first reaction wasn't shock, but laughter. He said he knew I hadn't done anything too bad, because he never thought me capable of a felony. He decided to ride his motorcycle to the station to see the action. By the time he got there, our parents had been called and Ken and I fingerprinted and released to our parents without being charged. Bobby recalled later that the police station was abuzz with laughter at the sad scene Ken and I had played out for the entertainment of the entire squad; we were the talk of the police station for weeks.

Uncle Bobby (Sheriff Deputy Robert Helms) on his motorcycle

The ride home with Pop was intense and silent; he was as angry as I'd ever seen him. Pop took pride in his reputation and told me repeatedly that integrity was the most important attribute in a person. Later that afternoon, I would receive my last spanking from Pop. We both hated it, but we knew I deserved it.

Ken and I were not technically arrested—no record exists. Although Ken observed my heist, we had no plan to steal anything when we walked into McCrory's. I'm sorry I made him an accomplice to a thief. He forgave me quickly, but I find it easier to laugh about the episode than he does.

Freshman Performist

Ham

I am a ham—always have been. The first show I was featured in took place when I was three and opened New Year's Day at dawn with a one-boy, pajama-clad parade down Warnell Street, cranking out noisemaker pandemonium.

I was always verbose and was renowned (or renounced) for my gift of gab. As a post-toddler, I was a decent singer. I mastered "Teddy Bear's Picnic" by listening to it on the radio several times and sang it to friends and strangers, with no prompting necessary. I also sang it to myself with great gusto and a few dance steps.

Me doing Stan Laurel

In anticipation of starting kindergarten, I learned the chorus to "Heigh Ho, Heigh Ho, It's Off to Work We Go." I began singing it "straight" as Mama drove me to Hiawatha's tribe. Over the course of a few weeks, I had progressed to singing it in dwarf character as Sneezy (with several "achoos" and sniffles), Grumpy (frowning with arms crossed in anger) and

Sleepy (with yawns and stretches). My mother particularly liked Sleepy. On the way to kindergarten one day, she pulled over so that she could better appreciate my drowsy dwarf imitation. I finished the last line of the song by pretending to fall asleep. The car rocked with laughter. Her laughter made me giggle, and that made her laugh even harder. We got even sillier from there.

I sang to myself a great deal when I was seven or eight. I knew the words to "How Much Is that Doggie in the Window?," "The Ballad of Davy Crockett," and "The Mickey Mouse Club March." When I heard any of those songs on the radio or TV, I joined in with my countertenor voice. Walking to or from school, I'd find myself humming a song and gradually begin to sing it. I delighted in making my own music, but I was aware that it got on some folks' nerves, so I stopped at the first sign of disapproval.

My early hamming-it-up routine with a dapper, slouching movie star stance

Throughout elementary school, my teachers consistently reported me as "talkative" or "overly talkative"—I believed speech was a performance method as well as a way to communicate.

Euterpe (Greek Goddess of Music and Song)

Unlike homework or baseball practice, I enjoyed memorizing the lyrics and melody and practicing a song. My natural key is C major, and although I have no claim to perfect pitch, I can hit middle B consistently without benefit of a reference tone.

My sister and I performed three seasons of Christmas pageants when I was in elementary school to a small parental audience; all three shows were monster hits. Like many professional theater people, we didn't much like each other, but we worked well together and enjoyed the shared rave reviews.

**Me talking and Judy ignoring me the best she can,
with me blind to her rejection**

In junior high school, I played in the band—well, not so much in it as at it. I had terrific sax fights with Robbie, and

Ralph and I drew an appreciative crowd in the school yard with our beatnik fights. Judy and I watched Dick Clark's TV teen dance show *American Bandstand* without fail on weekday afternoons after school. We danced, but separately. On a couple of occasions, Judy tried to teach me how to fast dance to rock and roll, but since we were reluctant to touch each other, that didn't work.

Terpsichore (Greek Goddess of Dance)

Learning to twist in front of a full-length hall mirror changed everything. I practiced for hours, until the whole family begged me to stop playing Chubby Checker's record. I got well beyond acceptable at twisting and discovered dancing made me as happy as singing. I also knew girls liked good dancers, so, between the joy of frolic and the potential for having girls like me, I was a convert to Terpsichore.

I made my twist debut at the Planteen, a city-run youth center on Dort Street, where they held dances most weekends. Pop tunes and rock songs played until 10 or 11 p.m. I enjoyed arriving early and visiting with the staff and chaperones, whom I knew well; a couple of the ladies were members of my parents' bridge club. On several occasions, I helped them with housekeeping chores so we'd have time to play a hand of canasta before the doors officially opened.

Once the girls arrived, I turned my attention away from the chaperones and toward the dance floor, the music, and the young ladies sitting along the far wall. I knew them all and was comfortable initiating a conversation, even if they were reluctant to engage. I talked with the guys too, but that wasn't the point of the dance. To me dance was only a verb and not a noun. I didn't go to "the dance," I went *to* dance. I enjoyed dancing with a variety of girls in different age groups, but I was intuitively drawn to the best dancers.

My method of flirting with girls was to charm them as best I could with an outrageous exaggeration that was between just the two of us. I would claim, for example, I was an atheist, with a sheepish smile that ran counter to my claim. I then built on that comment, constructing a make-believe story around the deceit. Frequently, devices such as asking (with a wink and a nod) a girl to marry me or to be my girlfriend created an intimacy that we could enjoy in its absurd insincerity.

I made my flirtations as a private joke and respected the individual nature of the flirtation. I stopped or changed course if I sensed any sign of discomfort. I used a wide variety of nicknames for girls, such as Honey, Babes, Tiger, Bunny, and Silly. I avoided using the same contrivance with more than one girl. I sought nuance in the spontaneity of the individual give-and-take. The more she responded in good humor, the better the fun.

My dancing was smooth. I wasn't the best male dancer in the room, but I was accomplished, having learned the latest dance moves from *Bandstand*. I no longer needed to dance in front of a mirror; it was coming naturally. I heard there was a "black Planteen" across the railroad tracks, and although I was curious, I never attempted to find out about it.

I found partners who danced with abandoned joy to be irresistible, regardless of any other factors. My slow dancing was marginal, but I enjoyed the intimate warmth of holding a girl; it was like hugging while walking. I was enamored with the twist and subsequent dances like the frug, dog, monkey, pony, hitchhiker, and my specialties, the watusi and the mashed potatoes. I knew I was good enough and therefore didn't worry about how I looked or what others thought—it was animated merriment for the duration of the song—especially a rock and roll song with a strong bass line and a stompin' back beat.

In high school, I continued to dance frequently at the Planteen and began dating different girls for varying stretches. A date might include a drive-in movie, but almost always involved dancing. There were some dances at school, but the most popular spot was the Palladium in Lakeland, about 30 minutes east of Plant City. I would become a regular.

Thalia (Greek Goddess of Theatric Comedy and Festivity)

In my freshman year, I joined the mixed chorus. As a result, I landed a supporting role in the school musical *Brigadoon*, by Lerner and Loewe. The time-traveling love story takes place in Scotland and New York City. My character was Andrew MacLaren, the gruff, stern father of the two female leads, Fiona and Jean. I had a few lines.

The Brigadoon cast rehearsing

The night went very well—except perhaps for the celebration after the show. I was inexperienced with alcohol; I'd had a few beers and sneaked some of Pop's liquor on a few occasions, but that was the extent of my drinking. When the play was over, Gene (who was the play's lead) and I joined some other guys and drove for a few hours in the countryside outside of Plant City. We rode the two-lane blacktop telling jokes, singing to the radio, and talking about girls. There were four of us in Gene's car, and we had a case of Falstaff beer. I got intoxicated, but not overly so. I liked the feeling, and the other guys were more fun than I had noticed before. It was a splendid night, and I got home before midnight without incident.

On closing night, we had another superb show, with a standing ovation and curtain calls. Our excitement about the adoration we received from the hometown crowd of parents and friends persisted well after the audience had left, beyond changing out of our costumes and the darkening of the auditorium. Several of the lads got into cars and began another country drive as a reprise of the preceding night's shindig. I again rode with Gene.

Instead of Falstaff, we had two pints of sloe gin—made from a bitter-tasting plum that the English favor. I'm not English. To say I overdid it misses the mark. I should have gotten sick, but I didn't have the sense of a seasoned sot to do so. The first hour was fun; the last may have been, but I have no recollection of it. I got home before midnight again but had to be carried to the front door. I made it to the sofa on my own.

The house was quiet. I evidently wasn't, and my snoring woke Pop about 2 a.m. When he saw my condition, he helped me to the bathroom and got me to throw up. He took me to bed and laid me on my back. He never confronted me about my behavior that night. Perhaps my near-death hangover the next day led him to extend grace to me by not speaking about my first drunken binge. Or maybe my performance behind the footlights gave me some extra credit. More likely, he was at a loss as to how to discipline me for being a boy who was growing up and taking his first bitter taste of becoming a man and the consequences of that.

Eris (Greek Goddess of Discord)

In 1962, I quit the choir at First Methodist Church. Although I enjoyed the church services, respected the pastor, had many friends there, and loved singing in the choir, there was trauma within the church, locally and nationally. Church had become less spiritual for me. Methodists were wrestling with integration. The clergy largely was for it, while the laity was mostly for segregation of races—within not just the church, but society. My family sided with the Plant City congregation against integration; I wasn't so sure I did.

Our pastor supported integration, but he was transferred and replaced by a clergyman who did not support it. The Methodist Church bishops and district superintendents were consistent in their condemnation of segregation, but they were unwilling to back up their official statements with substantive action.

From the choir stall, looking out at parishioners, I could see the tension in the pews. It wasn't just that attendance was down; there were fewer smiles on people's faces, and they sang with less emotion. A couple of the adults in the choir resigned. I didn't consult with anyone about my decision to quit the choir. My grandparents, mother, and sister attended church regularly, but Pop did not. I had no relationship with the new pastor, so I just stopped going to choir practice. I still attended Sunday services, but not regularly.

The Plant City High School mixed chorus was a delightful alternative to church choir, but I missed the large pipe organ directly behind the choir and hymns like "Amazing Grace" and "How Great Thou Art." More importantly though, black gospel music had found its way into my bedroom a couple of years earlier. I was a regular listener of spirituals on the radio and had learned the lyrics and melodies to many of them. I found them a powerful form of religious music and sang them with at least as much vigor as I had the hymns of the Methodist Church.

Gelos (Greek God of Laughter)

Examining my freshman yearbook, I found that of the 44 entries (excluding such messages as "Best wishes"), seven classmates referred to me as a "nut." "Good sense of humor" was noted five times, "sweet" four times, and "funny" three. I tried to avoid being foolish or giddy, preferring the absurd and—hopefully—witty; I was less Jerry Lewis or Buddy Hackett and more Jonathan Winters or Bob Newhart. I enjoyed a laugh or smile and strove for them, while observing the limits of my polite friends' tolerance and attention.

I had several comic bits in play my freshman year. My homeroom teacher, Mrs. Leggett, wrote in my annual, "To my boyfriend." I was able to pull a C average that year, despite my apathy. But I was making friends with some good people, and girls liked me.

My classmate Trina wrote in my freshman yearbook, "You have the best sense of humor I have ever known." She included a postscript: "I didn't really think you were an atheist (at heart that is)." I recognize the risk in reading too much into an off-the-cuff comment of a young teen, and, although I'm flattered she thought so highly of my sense of humor, her reference to my joking about being an atheist reveals I was stepping away from formal religion.

I've never been an atheist, but I have always been skeptical of religion under any banner. It was about the time she wrote her comment that I dropped out of the church choir. I became more irreverent as the conflict within the church intensified. The spiritual appeal of black gospel music remained part of me.

Sneakin'

Cats sneak; dogs watch, listen, and bark. There is no such thing as a dog burglar. I am more feline than canine. As a very young boy, I was a match thief. I would sneak up on a matchbook, pocket it, and wait for my chance to finish it off. I once managed to set a sofa on fire. In elementary school, I developed sneaking and pouncing skills on the playground. I was a sneaky BB gun sharpshooter. I sneaked Pop's cigarette butts and tried my hand at smoking. I sneaked upstairs to the attic to cheat with my mother's teaching materials.

Joyride

....

I am 13, and I sneak off with my mother's car to Lakeland, several miles from our house. It is late afternoon on a weekday, and the rest of the family will be gone for at least three hours. I take my mother's spare car keys from the kitchen dish. From there, nothing much is required of me to take my first real drive. After confirming I have plenty of gas, I set out on the newly completed section of Interstate 4 between Plant City and Lakeland.

I decide to stop at the new McDonald's on Memorial Boulevard for a burger and a Coke. The stoplights along the two-lane boulevard require my full attention. At McDonald's, I park the Ford away from other cars without issue and go inside. No one questions me my about my age—I'm a tall kid. I decide to return to Plant City via U.S. Highway 92 so I can experience a different road.

Me playing like I'm off in my mother's car at age 12

I head west on Memorial to Wabash Avenue and turn left to pick up U.S. 92. After only a block or so, I see it's getting late and that returning by the interstate would make more sense. I turn down Sterling Street; I plan to circle the block to get back on Memorial.

I realize after making a series of left turns, there's no way out of the neighborhood to Memorial, so I decide to turn around and retrace my path. I have every confidence in my ability to back up, even though the street is narrow, with open ditches lining both sides. I pull into the driveway of a house.

As I begin to back up, a car suddenly appears, heading toward my mother's car. I attempt to pull back into the driveway and miss—by the narrowest of margins. The car takes a pronounced and violent dip to the right. With effort, I'm able to get the door open. Examining my situation, I see that the left wheels are three inches off the ground and the right wheels rest at the bottom of the ditch. There does not appear to be any damage to the car.

Climbing back inside, I try to drive the car out of the ditch, with no luck at all. I go to the rear and try pushing it out; I'm now becoming frenzied. Sitting on the trunk, I consider my options. I can go to one of the houses on the street, call home, beg for help, and take my punishment. Or, I could, perhaps, maybe . . . As I try to complete that thought, I look across the street. Two doors down, there is a wrecker in the driveway.

I knock on the door and a young man answers. As he opens the door, he looks over my shoulder and sees the auto all askew in the ditch across the street. His first words are, "Need some help?" I am speechless, a very rare thing. I finally get out a squeaky, "Yes, please, sir." Not only does the wrecker driver pull the Ford out of the ditch in less than five minutes, he refuses my offer of the little cash I have. He tells me to get going. I oblige with multiple thank yous. He waves goodbye; I wave back.

I make it home well before anyone in the family returns. No one is the wiser, but I know that I have used all of the luck life allows in stealing a car. I do not repeat that act.

Nighthawk

My bedroom is stifling, and I suffer from insomnia and boredom. After Pop sets up the coffee percolator with Maxwell House coffee ("good to the last drop") for the next morning and turns off the lights, I play like I'm going to bed and wish him goodnight. I go to my bedroom, turn the radio down low, and listen to "race music" until I'm sure everyone is asleep. I sneak to the living room slowly and silently. With all the lights off, I stealthily close the hall door to the bedrooms, turn on our only TV, and tune in to Jack Paar with Hugh Downs. I keep the volume very low, sit on the floor next to the TV, and enjoy a night of comedy and commentary. Pop often tells me, "Nothing good happens after midnight"; I am not convinced, and, even if he is right, the summer-heated boredom is oppressive. I become a regular Friday night viewer.

I exercise excellent control stifling my laughs or smothering them with my hand. I head to bed once the show is over—test patterns are more boring than my bedroom ceiling. That works for several months, but Pop catches me one night and I get a lecture about being up past midnight.

I know my friend and neighbor, Gene, is similarly hooked on Jack Paar, and we often compare our impressions of the latest broadcast. Gene is three years older and has few constraints on his curfew. I discuss my dilemma with him, and he asks if I'd like to come to his house to watch Jack Paar.

A few days later, I wait until my house is dark and quiet, carefully unlock the two hook latches to the screen on my bedroom window, and quietly climb down. Gene's house is a block away, and I encounter no problem. I repeat this a few times a month and get very good at it.

We start a tradition of eating hot dogs during the program. We boil up franks during commercials and eat them on white bread with yellow mustard that comes out of a flatulent plastic bottle that always makes us laugh. I leave around 1:30 a.m. As I grow older, I sneak off to Gene's to watch Carson twice a month or so. I am careful not to spoil my after-midnight forays by sneaking out too frequently or becoming sloppy in my technique. This goes on for several years.

Mark Time

We are to meet again at the corner of West Cherry and North Ferrell streets. It's a few minutes before midnight when I crawl out of my window. As I begin the mile-and-a-half walk, it's very still, except for the crickets and a lone automobile in the distance. It is possible to hear a car several blocks away after midnight in a small town and see the reflection of its headlights on trees and homes from even farther. Even though there's no traffic, I avoid the main through streets, preferring the streets with lots of stop signs, I walk on the grass and stay off paved road surfaces or sidewalks—it's quieter.

Me at my sneakin' peak

I get there early, the walk having taken just a little over half an hour. I step behind the designated tree. The oak tree canopy makes Cherry Street very dark, and I hear

Mark before I see him, even though he's walking softly. As we greet, he hands me one of the two Coke bottles he's holding. Even in the faint light, I can see it has about two ounces of liquid in the bottom—tonight, it's whiskey. I had brought the drinks from Pop's cabinet last time, and Mark takes some pleasure in reducing his dad's stock for our treat tonight. We toast each other and take a sip.

We walk south on Ferrell Street as a train comes through town. It is a long one, inbound to Tampa. The whistle, the track crossing bells, and the rumble of the train itself are sufficient to allow us to speak in conversational tones rather than our usual whispers for several minutes. We begin talking about our previous midnight sojourn.

We'd been invited by two girls to visit them at a house with a detached one-bedroom apartment, where they were spending the night. We accepted and got there around one a.m. Both girls are ninth graders, a year younger than we are. Mark was interested in the girl who invited us. Although I knew who the other girl was, I'd never spoken to her. They are both attractive, but Mark's date more so. There was laughing, dancing, and a bit of romance. It was a memorable night.

We stop talking as we approach Ferrell Street turning into Whitehall. We know there are two always alert guard dogs at a house we are approaching—they sleep tied up in the yard and are barking monsters. We slow our pace and move as silently as possible. We slip past the house and reach the bay head—a swampy area where bay laurel dominates. There are no homes on either side of the road.

This stretch of our walks is the darkest, and from this spot, we can see the Milky Way. We stop and admire at our leisure, then resume our conversation in good cheer. Mark begins, "Last month's walk was the best." I agree that of the half-dozen we'd had, none compared to our trip to "the apartment." Mark declares, "I really like my date from the apartment, and I've started asking her out."

As we approach McLendon Street, we stop and discuss whether we should visit Trey, whose house is a block away. He lives with his grandmother and is the smartest and coolest guy I know. Even though he's a year younger, he too enjoys staying up late. We approach Trey's house and see the light on in his bedroom, which faces the street. We knock gently on his window. When he sees us, he motions us to go to the back door. He lets us in and leads us to his bedroom, and we listen to a newly released album Trey had purchased earlier that week, *The Freewheelin' Bob Dylan*.

Mark and I are familiar with Dylan from his first album the year before, but neither of us has heard this new one. Beginning with "Blowin' in the Wind," we are captivated. The songs, largely written by Dylan, include "A Hard Rain's A-Gonna Fall" and "Don't Think Twice, It's All Right." The album is full of humor (which Trey generously explains at a couple of points) and is certainly political, but it is enigmatic, too. Trey tells us the subtlety is intended. We had planned a quick conversation with him, but we don't leave until we've played the vinyl in its entirety.

We wish Trey goodnight and continue our walk. The moon has risen since we got to Trey's. Mark and I prefer moonlit nights, in part because it makes us more alert. Tonight feels different after listening to Dylan.

"Blowin' in the Wind" stays with us, and, walking toward the library, we feel a light wind at our backs. The stillness of familiar surroundings that bustle during the day is peaceful. The night's shade drawn on things most see in the bright Florida sunshine has created an ideal setting for us to ponder and discuss Dylan's questions about freedom and peace. Mark and I wish each other good night once we get back to Courier Field. It was a terrific sneak.

Done In

I walk carefully along the north side of our house. It is late even for me—after three a.m. I watched the *Tonight Show* with Gene and then took a walk by myself around the neighborhood behind the cemetery. I am sleepy but noiseless. I make it to the screen door of the back porch and remove my shoes. I climb the three steps in slow motion and gently lift the handle to the door I left open earlier. My first step is tricky; there is a loose board on the wooden floor that creaks loudly, and I slowly step over it and shift my weight from my rear foot to my front foot— not a sound.

The back porch is very dark, but I am so practiced I could walk the last few feet with my eyes closed. I creep past where I know the washing machine is on my left and the porch dining table on my right and reach for the doorknob. I turn it slowly and push gently—nothing. I turn the knob the other direction and push again, harder.

Suddenly, a hand firmly grabs my shoulder from behind. I jump and almost fall—I forget to breathe, my legs tremble, and I shudder. "The door is locked, Jim" booms from the dark.

My omniscient Pop

Pop scared me more than he intended. He tells me to sit down at the porch dining table. He sits down too and lights up a cigarette so I see him plainly. He looks a bit angry but is mostly concerned that he scared me so badly. I've been nailed, and we both know it. I have been sneaking out for a few years. I can't make eye contact.

Pop says, "Jim, I know you've been sneaking out for months." That added to my shock. "I didn't stop you because I trust your judgment, but lately you've been gone entirely too long and I think it's affecting your schoolwork. It must stop. Tonight."

He continues, "You know how I feel about staying out past midnight. You must stop sneaking out. If you agree to use the front door, I'll let you stay out until midnight. You have to tell Gene that, too. Do you agree?" I do.

....

I continued to sneak.

Sophomoric Sensations

Showtime

I joined the "Stardusters" my sophomore year. It was a choral group of about 25 boys and girls who sang well. Our repertoire was pop tunes mostly from the 1940s and early 1950s, such as "Moon River," "Fly Me to the Moon," and, predictably, "Stardust." We performed at school events, nursing homes, and local churches and did some Christmas caroling from the back of a pickup truck. The singing was delightful, and it was sedate fun. I made friends with several members.

The 1963 Stardusters (me, back row with eyes closed)

As a result of that gig, I was selected for a role in the high school's musical comedy, *Calamity Jane*, later in the year—that would not be as decorous an affair. The play was set in the Old West town of Deadwood in the late 1800s. My character was Francis Fryer, a song and dance man from back East who was hired by the Deadwood Golden Garter Saloon owner, who mistakenly thought he was hiring a woman performer, Frances. With a cast and crew approaching 100, it was a big production. We were led by Mr. Herbert Beam, and several faculty members were on the production staff. Although it was not professional theater, we worked hard to make it a class show.

The plot is a love story between Wild Bill Hickok and the overpowering, six gun-toting "Calam." There are several mistaken identities in the story, including Fryer's. The show is based on the 1953 film *Calamity Jane* featuring Doris Day; it won an Oscar for Best Song—"Secret Love." The play never made it to Broadway, but there were regional and international productions. Martha Raye and Carol Burnett played the title character in early 1960s stage versions.

My first solo number was as the male Francis Fryer. I sang and soft-shoed my way through "Everyone Complains about the Weather." The song required me to sing, dance, sing again, and close with an extended dance. The song was a cinch, but I had to practice the steps and moves for hours. I was pleased with my improvement.

**Me as Francis Fryer speaking
to Ross, the student director**

My second number was as the female Frances Fryer. I was cross-dressing as a saloon-singing vamp from Chicago because the Golden Garter Saloon owner had promised his male patrons a female vaudeville performer. He was determined to deliver, even after he realized his mistake. My female masquerade required little dancing, but the song, "I've Got a Hive Full of Honey" offered an ideal opportunity to go to extremes. As a sophomore, I found that easy enough.

At the dress rehearsal, I practiced making two quick costumes changes from male song and dance man to femme fatale and back to vaudeville dandy. During rehearsals, I was so hurried that in the dim light of the wings, I inadvertently bumped into a stage fireplace placed there for the next scene. It fell on my right foot with much violence and noise. I was not badly injured, and I was able to finish my costume change and hit my spot back on stage in time for the downbeat as the rest of the cast laughed— which didn't bother me at all. In fact, I enjoyed it, since the play was a comedy, after all.

Both nights of the play, I nailed my soft-shoe and my singing was fine—the applause more so. There were no problems with the costume switches, and I looked forward to my second number.

In a striking yellow chiffon dress with large floppy hat, full makeup, and a long wig, I made a passingly attractive lady—tall with no bosom, but not bad. My voice was on the far side of changing from countertenor to baritone, but my falsetto was as strong as ever. The song's lyrics were perfectly risqué.

I got two wonderful arms
I got two wonderful lips
I'm over twenty one, and I'm free!
Oh, I've got a hive full o' honey
For the right kind of honey bee!

I sang the song well; some said perhaps too well—many thought I was singing to a recording by a woman—no laughs in that, but the lyrics helped establish the gag. I further compensated with my movements as Frances. I avoided the bump and grind, but I used my overly long arms seductively, shimmied, winked, blew kisses, and suggestively adjusted my bodice. I strolled among classmates who were playing the roles of cowboys, dance hall girls, and the cavalry at the Golden Garter Saloon, sat on the lap of one cowpoke, and flirted with the rest. The crowd loved it.

The after party the second night was terrific. The male lead (Wild Bill) was played by Larry. His dad and mine had been partners in a failed used car lot, and he and I had been in the previous year's production of *Brigadoon*. He had a fine voice and did great imitations. On the closing night, we joined a few other guys and drove 40 miles to Clearwater Beach, where we drank beer, reprised some of the songs from the play, and talked about girls. My pop thoughtfully left the door open and the lights on late that night—he said nothing about my being late the next day.

Sofia

I knew Sofia from the Methodist Church and the connection of both of our fathers working at the local Ford dealership. Her older sister, Judy, had been in the musical

Brigadoon with me the year before, and Sofia joined the chorus my sophomore year—she played one of the six dance hall girls in *Calamity Jane* and was the most attractive.

We made each other laugh, but it wasn't until high school that we started spending considerable time together. She was a year older, so other than chorus, we had no classes together. We started dancing to records together at the Planteen recreation center. We danced with others as well, but we knew we clicked on the dance floor.

Her dancing was better than mine, and she was much easier to look at. She danced as if she meant it to be fun regardless of the response—which ensured a favorable response. As the year passed, we danced to live bands at the weekly National Guard Armory dance. We owned the joint—others would routinely stop dancing around us and watch us (mostly Sofia) dazzle with smooth and closely matched moves.

Sofia and her younger courtier

We didn't practice our dancing—it was absolutely inspired spontaneity. Imagine a rhythm and blues rock group like the Four Tops dancing in half-time (slowing it down to half the speed of the actual tempo of the song), sliding the feet sideways from one foot to the other, stepping two steps back, crossing one leg over the other—then stepping forward. The knees are collapsed and the arms and hands active but loose. We turned often, and every time we faced, we broke into broad smiles.

The only touching was at the end of the song, when we hugged and thanked each other between laughs. At times, our movements and happiness in the moment were metaphysical—not every dance certainly, but at least once each night at the armory dances, we were transported to a different and exuberant reality, with good rock and roll as our soundtrack.

Court of Affection

With my best friend Kenny and Sofia's good friend "Tiger," we formed a court of teens. Our queen was Sofia, even though we didn't expressly acknowledge it at the time. Our mission was to amuse one another and advance our friendship. We began seeking each other out at school to talk and giggle. We had nicknames for each other. The court was open to others, but we were the principals. There was no charter; there were no royal meetings; there were no rituals—it was organic to its core, and it was delightful to be connected to trusted friends we were learning to love.

Sometime after the production of *Calamity Jane*, Sofia went to a revival at church. She invited me, but I demurred. She went three consecutive evenings and sought me out each of the following days to talk about her experience. On the last night of the revival, she joined a few other congregants in walking to the front of the church to announce her conversion. When she informed me, she was as happy as I'd ever seen her. I told her I was happy for her, but I was taken aback by the depth of her new religiosity.

In April 1963, I participated in a panel discussion for my world history class on the five principal religions of the world and their similarities to each other. I do not remember which religion I addressed, but it would have been fitting had it been "Blended."

Me on the far left looking my most skeptical

Sofia liked the nickname Kenny gave her—Bunny. Kenny and I thought being a "bunny"—a Hugh Hefner Playboy bunny—was a fun aspiration for Sofia. However, we knew Sofia would be highly successful thanks in some part to her beauty, but mostly due to her intellect and charm. The nickname made Sofia laugh, because she too knew she would do so much better than a cottontail.

When the school year ended, I took a summer job that reduced my opportunities to dance with Sofia. I also began going to dance venues outside of town. We still danced with the same intensity the few times that we saw each other at the Planteen that summer. Those were special occasions to celebrate.

Paradise

My first real job was at Paradise Fruit Company the summer before my junior year. My friend and neighbor Gene and I applied together and were hired on the spot. We started that weekend on the packaging warehouse assembly line. Paradise Fruit, based in Plant City, made candied fruit and peel mix for fruitcakes. Fruitcakes are deservedly the butt of jokes like, "How long do fruitcakes last? Until someone actually eats one." Johnny Carson quipped, "The worst Christmas gift is fruitcake...There is only one fruitcake in the entire world, and people keep sending it to each other, year after year." Ironically, my pop made a terrific fruitcake. It had more than enough liquor in it to kill the taste.

Our job was to push chunks of candied fruit through 20 or so 4-, 6-, or 8-ounce-sized holes in a stainless steel wheel into plastic containers fed automatically under the wheel's holes. It was a three-person operation, with two people pushing fruit through holes and one shoveling syrupy fruit from large barrels onto the center of the wheel.

Our third man was James. He had difficulty getting the right amount of fruit in the container, so he took on the role of "shoveler." James was not a good worker. Gene and I spent a good portion of our shift yelling at him to hurry; you could hear our cries of "James, come on" or "James, you're killing us" or "James, where are you?" ring across the warehouse.

Beyond us on the assembly line were six middle-aged women who weighed and inspected the containers now stuffed with candied fruit. The ladies were patient with us—we often held up the conveyor belt because we couldn't keep up.

The women would leave their stations and take over when we had to completely stop the stainless steel wheel. Gene and I tried to return their generosity by weighing and sealing the full plastic containers at the women's posts, but we were just not up to it. We drew laughter, not scorn, from the ladies who so outclassed us.

We were very sore after the first few days, but we stuck with it. The warehouse was unairconditioned and stifling. Gene and I finished our shift in the early afternoon exhausted and soaked with sweat.

The second week, Gene had an inspiration: we would go over to his girlfriend's house and swim in her parents' pool. Gene had been dating her for years and had open entry to the residence. We got there, changed into swim trunks, and dove in.

We also had unintended access to the liquor cabinet and partook. We had a drink, refilled the bottle with water, and floated a bit after our swim. The after-work cool-down couldn't have been better. We made decent wages and were dependable, if slow. By summer's close, our forearms resembled Popeye's, less the tattoos.

The Dynamic Visions

Gene started a band around that time—The Dynamic Visions. It was a rock band, and Gene was the lead singer. Buddy was on electric keyboard. I knew him from his participation in *Brigadoon*. Tommy, who I knew as a classmate and teammate in pickup football games, played electric bass. There were two fellows in the band I hadn't known before, Bob the drummer and Tom the lead guitar player. The band practiced hard and got very good quickly. The Visions played lots of soul music, and Gene did a terrific stage show in the tradition of James Brown— including wearing a cape and falling on his knees.

The Dynamic Visions
(left to right: Bob, Tom, Tommy, Gene, and Buddy)

Gene began playing gigs on weekends in the Plant City area at school dances, teen clubs, and VFWs. I became a Visions roadie that summer and cut back my routine of going to dances at the Planteen and the National Guard Armory.

Junior Underachievement – Part 1

School

Singing in the Plant City High School Stardusters chorale for a second year was fun. Dub, my good friend since kindergarten, joined the choir, and his presence improved the singing and increased the laughter. I also joined the Forensic League that year and—probably because of the small size of the team—was elected president. We participated in several debates across Hillsborough County and gave speeches to the student population in the auditorium.

The school did not produce a musical that year, but I had the lead in a two-show performance of a play for the Future Teachers of America—very few guys tried out for the role. I would have preferred to sing and dance, but the show had some comedy mixed in with its more serious message about education—not the best typecasting, that last part. I went to class regularly but dispassionately, and I cut class irregularly but with enthusiasm. I was a C student.

Me on stage in a play celebrating American Education Week

JFK

....

Sofia picks up Kenny, Tiger, and me in front of the high school around 7 a.m. School has been cancelled for the day, so we set off immediately. It is early enough that, even with the heavy security on Grand Central and the crush of downtown Tampa traffic, we are parked only a block away from the 28-mile-long motorcade route.

Kenny and I are sitting on top of the back seat of the convertible, taking turns waving the large Dixie flag with hoots and rebel yells. Tiger and Sofia are standing in front on the floor board, matching us in enthusiasm, and Tiger is waving a smaller Stars and Stripes. The crowd around us is curious about the teenagers in a red 1962 Ford Galaxy celebrating the Confederate South. But in November of 1963, the South is firmly Democratic, so it isn't unusual to see teenagers in rebel character here supporting the young President.

President Kennedy is a rock star to all four of us, and we are giddy at the thought of seeing him in person. We also appreciate that he didn't go to war with the Soviet Union the previous year during the Cuban missile crisis and get us all killed.

We have grown up practicing what to do when the atom bombs fall. In grade school, we dropped under our desks (that would certainly do the trick), covered our heads, and curled up into tight little balls of burning flesh—only we didn't practice the burning flesh part. We had similarly futile drills in junior high. The drills stopped in high school; as we approach adulthood, we seem to have become more expendable. None of us has nightmares about imminent death by atomic holocaust, nor do our families have fallout shelters. But we all hear, "Tomorrow or the next day, life on the planet will end." Some might hear "may" rather than "will," but that is quibbling. My generation accepts that instant death from nuclear warfare is imminent and all hope is lost.

President Kennedy is in Tampa to tour MacDill Air Force Base—a prime target for U.S.S.R. missiles, given its proximity to Cuba and the base's inventory of nuclear-equipped bombers. It is the year before the next presidential election, but JFK is only polling a little better than 50 percent approval in the South, even though it is solidly Democratic. JFK lost Florida by 60,000 votes in 1960 to Nixon, so his visit is political, in part. We are visiting Tampa to see the charismatic president who has mesmerized us with his intellect, youth, charm, wit, and his wife—plus, he hasn't gotten us killed.

Although we don't get to shake his hand, we are close enough to do so. First Lady Jackie isn't with him, but he stands in his convertible and waves in our direction, and that is plenty good enough. We return to Plant City intoxicated from seeing a sitting president—this one in particular. He will be shot four days later in Dallas riding in the same limousine.

Our court of four never talks about the assassination, yet we grieve deeply—our trip to Tampa has sealed our relationship with each other and Kennedy.

....

Flop

In December 1957, two months after the U.S.S.R. launched Sputnik I, appearing to be winning the race to space, the United States responded by launching a Vanguard Test Vehicle Three missile from Cape Canaveral. It rose four feet off the ground, lost thrust, and fell back to earth. Its fuel tanks ruptured in a fireball, destroying the rocket and damaging the launch pad extensively. It was a spectacular flop.

Joe was short, red-haired, and good-hearted, but also a spectacular flop. His social skills were frightful in their awfulness.

....

Joe is there when Gene, my friend and driver, and I arrive at the second floor apartment in the Lakeland, Florida suburbs. He is standing by himself in the crowded kitchen. He has already worked the room, and the survivors are gaining distance. It is a dance party, with lots of Falstaff beer and a good mix of girls and guys. Several of my good friends from Plant City are there, having fun. The next record is Marvin Gaye's "Hitchhike." I join in and am welcomed by the girl hosting the party. I lose track of Joe— which most people who know him learn to do.

The dancing intensifies as the Falstaff is replenished. It is after midnight, but few are leaving. Joe walks into the living room/dance floor, where all the furniture is against the walls. He places a case on a table and brings out a clarinet. Several couples stop dancing. Joe puts the reed to his lips and starts playing "Greensleeves," an Irish folk song that beginners often attempt. There is nothing rock and roll to be found in that number. Joe labors through the song, and he's a long way from acceptable. There is no applause. A guy yells out, "Do some James Brown!" Joe replies, "That's the only song I know."

As a couple of boos ring out, I walk up to Joe and ask if he would like to go outside with me. Joe says, "Oh, sure, James." I ask him to grab his case and escort him to the landing on the stairs between the ground and the second floor. He sits down and, looking up at me, asks, "What now?" I tell him, "Joe, just take a break for a few minutes. Would you like a beer?" He replies, "James, that would be great—that song did wear me out." I leave him, pick up two Falstaffs from the closest cooler, and give them both to him. He thanks me.

I return to the party, and Joe doesn't. The crowd is beginning to thin. I go to the open front door and see Joe stretched out on the landing. He has the dry heaves; people leaving the party have to step over him to get downstairs. A few grumble, one girl asks if he's okay, and another nudges him with her foot. He doesn't respond to any of these stimuli, but since he's still heaving—albeit with his eyes closed—I know he's okay. I prop him up and return to the party for a few more dances and a final beer.

Gene and I decide to leave, and we wish Joe goodnight as we step over him. He doesn't respond. We get halfway to Gene's car when I realize I've left my Winston cigarettes in the apartment. I tell Gene I'll be right back.

As I approach the stairs, I can see Joe is still lying on the landing, but no one else is around. He suddenly gets up, dusts himself off, picks up his clarinet, and skips down the steps. I am shocked at the miraculous recovery from his drunken stupor. He wishes me goodnight with a big smile as he walks by me. I do the same and walk up the first flight of stairs. On a hunch, I reach down and lift the two beer cans I gave him earlier. One is half full, the other not even open. He may have been a flop musically, but his passed-out sick act has been flawless. Having all those folks acknowledge and step over him clearly pleases him, even with his eyes closed.

....

My friends and I tried hard not to be cruel to Joe, but he made that a challenge. Gene and I were driving to Daytona Beach one morning, and we had both forgotten that Joe had asked to come along.

About 90 minutes into the three-hour drive, I started talking about an earlier incident in which Joe had committed a social faux pas. Gene laughed and told me about a similar incident involving Joe.

We heard a cough from the back seat and suddenly remembered Joe was there. He hadn't said a word or made a sound for the entire drive. I tried to apologize, but he cut me off, saying he enjoyed the stories. I knew he was being sincere about listening to words—almost any words—involving him. That's as close as we came to being cruel. Joe was a kind, sweet fellow, but too often he was toilsome to be around.

Continued in Junior Underachievement – Part 2

Part Six – Teen

Junior Underachievement – Part 2

Gainesville

....

Plant City High School has a superb basketball team in 1964, with 18 wins and 6 losses in the regular season. We've won both the first and the second round tournaments, and we're advancing to the state tournament. It is Friday afternoon, after the pep rally. Sofia is driving, Tiger riding shotgun, Kenny behind Tiger, and me behind Sofia. The night is clear and cool, the ragtop of the Ford is down, and the three-and-a-half hour drive north promises to be a rollicking time, with the radio cranked up and all of us singing along.

Plant City High School pep rally for state championship basketball game (1964)

As we pass Leesburg, Florida, Sofia suddenly swerves to the left and slams on the brakes. I hear a resounding thud and feel the tires roll over something large. The car careens farther to the left. I see from the headlights that we've stopped just inches from a large tree. The car is still running. No one speaks for a few seconds, but the silence is broken by wailing and groans behind us. We've hit a dog—he's dying. We pile out of the car and walk a few yards back to the poor dog, a white German shepherd.

A man walking toward us from a house beside the road begins to run, screaming, "Roger!" As he nears us, he whispers, "Roger?" He bends down, lifts Roger in his arms, and asks if we are okay. Roger's breathing is labored, and his moans have become softer and less frequent. Sofia is crying but manages to say, "He came out of the bushes, and I am so sorry, so sorry." Tiger is crying too as she puts her arm around Sofia's shoulders. "Can we take him to a vet?" Kenny asks. The man turns and says, "It's too late for that." He takes Roger to the front of the house and lays him down on the grass close to the front porch. Roger is quiet now. I am tearing up, and Kenny is crying.

Sofia offers Roger's owner $50. The owner introduces himself as Mr. Sullivan and declines with a thank you. I ask if there is anything we can do. Mr. Sullivan says, "No" in a quiet voice as he begins sobbing. Roger is no longer breathing, but Mr. Sullivan continues to stroke his head. Mr. Sullivan says, "You should be on your way."

Our very somber court heads back to the Ford, still running with the lights on. Kenny is driving as we begin again. The top is now up, the radio off, and the cabin eerily still. Tiger is sitting in the front passenger seat, weeping softly. Sofia and

I are in the back seat, holding hands as she cries and dabs her eyes with her other hand.

Arriving about 8 p.m., we find Judy's dorm, and she's standing out in front with her roommate Pat. Two guys are with her, her boyfriend Charlie and his roommate Davis. Kenny stops in front of the dorm and lets me out after a protracted and melancholy goodbye. I hug Judy and Pat. Davis hugs me as we are introduced and, after some hesitation, Charlie does too.

We pile into Davis' nearby car, a beautiful beast—a 1954 Buick Roadmaster—black as coal with chrome bumpers and white sidewalls, a continental kit, and even an exterior sun shade. It is in fine shape and is a statement in 1950s Fireball V8 power and shiny beauty.

Judy and her friends are in high spirits but can see something is wrong with me. They ask how my trip was, and I tell them about Roger. Judy and I are sitting in the back seat. She suddenly puts her arm around me and gives me a deep, long hug. We shed a few tears.

Six more of Judy's friends meet us outside a club in Gainesville. Charlie takes me aside and tells me to let everyone else in our party go in and make sure I am the last in line. As the group works its way past the woman managing the door, Charlie makes sure he is in front of me.

As I try to pass, the woman stops me and asks for my ID. Charlie yells, "Hey gang, wait." The other ten folks stop, turn in our direction, and begin to back out of the club. The woman looks at the large group and waves us all in.

Next morning Davis takes me to the University of Florida gym where I find Tiger and Kenny, who, with Sofia, are staying at a small motel outside of town. They tell me Sofia is not up to coming to the game. Plant City wins its first game against Riviera High School 52–48 in overtime, and I'm sure our cheering helped their efforts. We will play in the State Class A Championship tomorrow against Seabreeze.

Next day, Sofia, Kenny, Tiger, and I meet again at the university gym for the state finals. We find good seats, and the game is a back-and-forth affair. We seem to be getting past the death of Roger, but it's all a bit forced.

The 1964 Planters basketball team in a huddle

We have a lead in the second half, but it's lost as the game is ending. We lose by eight points. Sofia, Tiger, Kenny, and I needed that win as much as the players. The drive back to Plant City is solemn; Sofia takes a 15-mile detour to avoid the Leesburg area. We get home safely and go our separate ways.

....

Our trip to Gainesville was bittersweet. The joy of the first part of the drive until Roger's death . . . witnessing Sofia's aching remorse. . . the reunion with and affection of my sister . . . meeting and partying with her friends . . . the thrill of the two ball games . . . coming so close to being state champions, only to lose at the end . . . the gloomy drive back.

Me as a junior underachiever

The Charities – Greek Goddesses
Aglaea (Splendor), *Euphrosyne* (Good Cheer), and *Thalia* (Festivity)

It was two weeks before the prom when I decided to go. Kenny and Sofia had been hounding me to go for weeks, but I wanted to go to Auburndale to see Gene and Tommy's band, The Dynamic Visions. They were playing a dance at the local American Legion, where I had met a cute girl months before. I was pretty sure she would be there to see The Visions. I gave in to Sofia, though, and decided to go to the prom.

I knew it was too late to get a date, and I didn't want to go stag. Tiger bailed me out by asking girls she knew, and she found a likely target—Sharon. Sharon and I had talked before at lunch and danced together several times at school dances. She was graceful, sunny, very pretty, but very young—a freshman. I cornered her in the hall and made my pitch about the prom.

It sounded a bit desperate to my ear, which surprised me, given my usual confidence and the fact that she was in the ninth grade and was likely to agree. She did, conditional on her parents' approval. The next day, she informed me her parents had said yes. I was pleased if not wildly excited. *(My indifferent approach to the prom was noted by the three Prom gods known as the Charities.)*

Pop had purchased a 1957 Thunderbird a few months earlier, soon after I got my driver's license. It was beautiful, fast, streamlined, and shocking pink, with a removable hard top. Pop had allowed me to drive it a few times, but always with him on the passenger side of the white leather bench seat. I asked him if I could borrow it for prom night, and he agreed and suggested I practice driving it. Everything was falling into place perfectly without much effort from me.

Me with Pop's '57 T-Bird in 1964

Over the next several days, I did little to prepare—I was busy practicing parking the T-Bird, and stuff was just taking

199

care of itself. I rented a dinner jacket and pants a couple of days before the prom, and my mother purchased a wrist corsage for Sharon and a boutonniere for me.

I started getting dressed at 6 p.m. on the night of the prom. (*The Prom gods frowned and commenced fire.*) My pants fit comfortably around my waist but were three inches too short. There was no time for an alteration, and the men's shop where I had rented the outfit was closed. I tried other pants, but they looked worse. I pulled the pants down as far as I dared on my hips, and the gap was a pronounced but not ridiculous two inches.

I wore Pop's longest pair of black socks so that little skin showed. I would just keep the coat buttoned so that folks couldn't see my low-riding trousers and try to avoid sitting down so my lower calf didn't show. My mother laughed when I came out of the bedroom and, after some discussion, agreed that there was nothing to be done. Thankfully, Pop didn't take any pictures. I was wearing my carnation and got $30 from Pop.

I said good night to my folks and walked to the driveway where the Thunderbird was waiting. Pop had filled it up and washed it shiny earlier that afternoon. As I opened the door, a bug flew into my ear. I slapped my ear harder than I intended, and ringing set in—a sonorous, high-pitched, pulsating tone. I could feel the bug staggering back out of my ear hole. It was probably dazed by the shock wave my slap produced. (*The Prom gods had sent me a messenger.*) It flitted off as I shook my head to clear it. That helped, but the ringing continued.

I slid in behind the wheel, started the mighty engine, put the T-Bird in reverse, and slowly backed out. At that moment, the shortness of my pants caught my eye. I backed into a palm tree—but not hard—and, upon inspection, could see only a little mark on the back fender. Luckily, my parents had gone back inside after waving goodbye from the front porch. I began again, making a note to ignore my bare exposed ankles the rest of the evening. The ringing continued.

I drove two miles to Sharon's house. As I parked in her driveway, I remembered the corsage sitting in my refrigerator. I was considering returning to pick it up, when her front door opened. It was Sharon's mom. I couldn't hear what she was saying because of the ringing. I turned off the T-Bird and waved to her. As I approached her, I began to understand what she was saying. "(garbled words) . . . we're repairing her zipper."

We introduced ourselves, and I was invited in. She asked me to sit on the sofa and served me a glass of Coke, which I put down on the glass coffee table. "(garbled words) . . . not there." I reached down, and my hand slipped, knocking the Coke and spilling a third of it onto the carpet. I apologized as she retrieved a dish towel to dab up my mess. She was speaking, but I could only understand about half of the words because of the ringing. I nodded a lot and apologized more. (The Prom gods were not placated by apologies.)

Sharon made a dramatic entry. As I stood up, I spilled the rest of the Coke on the sofa. Luckily, the dish towel was handy—as if Sharon's mom knew I wasn't done with fumbling the beverage. Her mother must have thought I was a complete dud: I couldn't make conversation because of my hearing impairment, and I spilled the same drink twice.

Sharon was gorgeous, and I told her so. Her mom took several pictures, and then we were off to the first prom for either of us. Sharon loved the Thunderbird. When I opened the door for her, she attempted to fold her long evening gown into the low-slung car while sliding in, which took a couple of attempts. Then I closed the door on the skirt of her dress. I apologized, and she laughed. I joined her—this show directed by the Prom gods was becoming a hilarious slapstick.

Sharon and the guy with the short trousers at the prom

Prom night for Sharon and me would be chock-full of bloopers, errors, and mishaps. I parked too close to another car, and Sharon couldn't get out on her side, so she tried to slide across to the driver's door but couldn't get past the steering wheel. I reparked the car well away from any other autos. We laughed throughout the process.

Walking up to the prom hall, I noticed that her dress was becoming unzipped. As a reflex, I tried to zip her up. She jumped, and I almost disrobed her. Facing me, she looked a bit angry and shocked, so I explained about her zipper. She smiled and started to giggle. I started laughing, and we exchanged a knowing look of how silly this whole thing was. (*Our laughter must have aggravated the Prom gods, because they doubled down.*)

We made it inside and found our table. We were the only couple at the table. Evidently, because we waited until the last possible moment, the caterer had to add a table for a single couple—us. Thankfully, my friends and their dates joined us as the night went on. We almost fell doing a slow dance, when I stepped on Sharon's hem. In the ladies room, the cold water faucet somehow came loose in her hand after she had put her long white gloves back on, and she couldn't turn the water off. (*The Prom gods had widened their target to include Sharon.*)

As we joined the buffet line, the Prom gods left for their dinner and caused nothing more consequential than a dropped fork at our table. We danced the rest of the evening; Sharon now dressed securely with safety pin assistance from Sofia and Tiger. We danced a few dances with others, trying to spread the foolishness around. When we left the prom, I folded her back into the T-Bird and drove her home without any interference from the Prom gods.

I walked her to her door, hugged her, and kissed her on her cheek. She said it was the strangest and most fun evening of her life. I agreed and turned to go.

As I did, I stepped on a cat sent from the Prom gods. The cat let out an otherworldly screech. Lights started coming on not only in Sharon's house, but across the neighborhood. We laughed until we cried. We said goodnight with warm smiles.

She wrote a note in my yearbook that year that confirms the great time we had, despite the displeasure of the Prom gods.

> *"James, I have known you just one year. This one year has truly been most rewarding for me. I will always remember our Prom date and all the fun. I honestly did enjoying going out with you."*

Sharon's note in my Junior yearbook

> *"Parting is such sweet sorrow. I really will miss you [sic] smiling face walking down the halls of PCHS next year. It will really break me up. Seriously, I have never had such fun as I had at the Prom. That I never will forget. I wish you all of the luck in the future. Always, Sharon"*

Sharon's note in my 1965 yearbook

My date with Sharon was a burlesque, but I've never known a better sport who laughed harder at the outrageous whimsies life throws our way.

Senior Weak

Shelly

....

It is lunch time, the first week of my senior year. I leave Plant City High School (PCHS) as soon as the bell rings and walk three blocks to the Strawberry Drive-In. I plan to be gone not only for the lunch period but for my Algebra 2 class as well. Shelly is outside the small drive-in, leaning on an empty car, smoking a cigarette. I light one up with my Pop's old Zippo lighter and, as I approach, wave with my first exhale.

She is dressed down as usual, but still striking. She nods back, coolly composed. She is one of the best dancers in school, and I always look forward to seeing, talking to, and dancing with her. She is edgy fun—I hope others say the same about me.

We haven't arranged a rendezvous—that isn't her style—but when I cut class for a burger, a shake, and a smoke, she is often there. Her eyes and mouth present a mischievous aspect full of mystery and amusement. She reminds me of Tinker Bell, the first crush of my earliest years.

She seems to care little about school, which I find alluring, given my own academic indifference. She is bright and quick, with a laugh that sounds like a tickle taken form. I try my best to make her laugh.

We talk little about school but rather music, upcoming dances, and classmates we enjoy or avoid, and why. She and I repeat this modest act of defiance several times this year. Our unplanned meetings are enhanced by their spontaneity.

....

Senior

I was re-elected president of the forensic league. I loved to debate and found winning an argument to be fulfilling. I learned that careful preparation and well-executed persuasion tools were a powerful combination. I wrote several speeches for my classmates in the forensic league and some for fellow students taking speech as a class. My going rate was three dollars, but I never charged the forensic league team.

The team did well in debate and speech competitions with other schools, and I took my modest leadership responsibilities seriously, for the most part. I also did my best to insure we all had fun in preparing and competing.

Me with the other officers of the PCHS forensic team

Civics

The first part of my senior year was largely about the national election. Most of my classmates had decided whether they supported southern Democrat Lyndon Johnson or conservative Republican Barry Goldwater from Arizona for president. I engaged in several debates, formal and informal, on the two candidates. Although I was sympathetic to the Republican view on the need for a limited federal government, I had changed my preference for president between the Florida Republican primary in May 1964 and the election.

My class and my friends were split on who to support in the 1964 presidential election

Pop had given up on the Democratic Party and become ultraconservative. He was fiercely anticommunist and often sympathetic to the position of the John Birch Society, an ultra-right political group whose leader supported Senator Goldwater. Pop gave me a book, *None Dare Call It Treason*, by John Stormer. He thought I would benefit greatly from its truth and insight. The author was a pastor and anticommunist.

First published in paperback in February 1964, it would have a hardcover printing in July and a total of 13 paperback printings by August. Over seven million copies were sold, making it the largest-selling political paperback book ever in America. The author said: "[Communists) have infiltrated every conceivable sphere of activity: youth groups; radio, television, and motion picture industries; church, school, educational, and cultural groups; the press; national minority groups; and civil and political units."

The first time I read the book, I was impressed. Its 236 pages included 800 references and footnotes—the book was full of frightening facts, and the weight of the footnotes gave it gravitas. One conspiracy anecdote Mr. Stormer used was President Franklin D. Roosevelt saying that some of his best friends were communists, with the Congressional Record cited as the source. I subsequently learned that, although the Congressional Record did contain Roosevelt's purported remarks on his friends being communists, the quote was actually from an essay written by a man who had been fired by FDR. The man did not reveal this supposed conversation with Roosevelt for 12 years, after the deaths of all the other people he claimed had been present. The book overflows with such misrepresentations and raw fabrications.

I deplored misinformation, and deception with made-up political facts outraged me. I began to think I needed to look beyond my family for political guidance. I knew I wanted the President Kennedy legacy continued. I was in favor of the 1964 Civil Rights Act that had passed in June of that year, with 80 percent of Republicans and 60 percent of Democrats in favor of the legislation. President Johnson had been instrumental in working it successfully through Congress. Senator Goldwater had voted against the Act and was very vocal in his opposition, based on his views on states' rights.

On September 7, 1964, the "Daisy spot" ad ran on national TV. It ran only once before it was pulled by Johnson's campaign, but it appeared on the nightly news programs and talk shows. It had a remarkable impact in its implication that Goldwater would start a nuclear war. It showed a young girl picking petals off a daisy. The image of the girl freezes, and the camera zooms in on the pupil of her right eye. The image then fades to a nuclear bomb explosion ending with the caption, "Vote for President Johnson on November 3." It was a devastating ad that helped assure Johnson's election.

Julie

My friendship with Julie developed over several years of being in home room together. She was a happy person. We began dating my senior year, and it was the best experience of that year. Julie, a cheerleader and competitive swimmer, was attractive, independent, and smart. She loved to kid around, and she was fun to dance with. I suspect we made a fine couple.

Julie in 1965

Over several months, I fell in love with Julie. We were well matched, our strengths and weaknesses complementing each other. I became more active in school events such as Friday night football games and home basketball games because of her role as cheerleader. We went to dances, but I didn't follow The Dynamic Visions as frequently. Julie and I understood our love and friendship would endure whether we ended up together or not.

The 1965 PCHS basketball team had another spectacular year with a second consecutive trip to the Florida State Championship finals. The team would finish the year with 21 wins and 8 losses, losing the state championship by two points. I had gone to the University of Florida my junior year for our school's unsuccessful first run at a state championship. I had great fun clubbing with my sister, who was in her senior year there, but now she and her friends had graduated. I wanted to attend a concert in Lakeland, so I got a full report of the game from Julie.

Barney

....

I really appreciate Pop's letting me borrow the '57 Thunderbird. I make good time driving to Dade City. The Dynamic Visions' outdoor concert starts on time, and Pyracantha Park is lovely, nestled up against the Pasco County courthouse. It is a beautiful Sunday afternoon under the oaks. I stay for the first set of rhythm and blues and decide to drive back the 30 miles to Plant City before it gets dark.

I open up the T-Bird as I pass through Zephyrhills on the southern border of Pasco County. I pass a slow-moving black sedan also going south, cross a single rail train spur, and floor it. The two-lane blacktop State Road 39 is deserted and extends to the horizon.

As I approach Crystal Springs, blinking red lights appear at a considerable distance in my rearview mirror. I decide to back off the accelerator as the flashy car gets bigger in my mirror. It doesn't look like a cop car; the red lights are on the dashboard. That's when I hear the siren.

I slow down more and pull off the road at the dirt entrance to a fenced field of cattle. The black car pulls in behind me. A Pasco County deputy sheriff is sitting in the driver's seat, and I can see him talking into his hand. He opens his door and yells out, "Stay in the car!" as he gets out of his car. He is very slight—skinny and short—and he reminds me of Barney Fife of the *Andy Griffith Show*. I think he must sit on a cushion to see over the dashboard.

His short legs take him a while to cover the distance between his unmarked car and the T-Bird. I fish out my license and the title from the glove box as he reaches my door. He asks, "Do you have any idea how fast you were going?" I wish him good afternoon and answer, "No sir." He continues, "112, and do you know you passed me in the no passing lane of a railroad crossing?" I repeat, "No sir."

"You will follow me back to Dade City, son," he commands. I try explaining we are in Hillsborough County and Plant City is much closer. He snaps back, "The crime occurred in Pasco, and that's where you're going." I make one last appeal: "Officer, my uncle is a sheriff's deputy for Hillsborough County—can't you please work with him in Plant City?" He almost hisses, "Follow me."

I follow him back to the Dade City courthouse I had left just a half hour before. The Visions are still playing. "Barney" leads me up the stairs to the second floor and escorts me into the booking room. I can hear The Visions starting their last set—I know the song list by heart.

Barney tells me to give him my keys and wallet, but I get to keep my belt. He has done this routine before and can easily spot a zero-risk-for-suicide criminal. Barney leaves without saying goodbye—the day is young, and he has a job to do. Another officer fingerprints me and takes a probably unflattering picture using a camera from the 1940s. A third officer takes me to one of two holding cells in the room. It is empty.

I ask him if I can make a phone call. He replies, "Later." I tell him, "Sir, my friends are playing that music you hear just outside. Would it be possible to get them a message explaining my situation?" He chuckles and walks away. I sit down on one of the four bunks as Gene begins the James Brown hit, "Try Me." I chuckle and see the officers across the room start to laugh, too.

Gene and The Dynamic Visions doing a James Brown number

212

The deputies and I enjoy the music. One of them asks about The Visions' history, and I give him a short summary. Once The Visions close their show, I'm allowed to call Pop. It takes him an hour to get to the courthouse. Barney brings in another perpetrator—this time, a DUI. The jail becomes very noisy when they put "Loud-Unsober" in the adjoining cell. Pop pays my bail, for which I am thankful.

One of the deputies tells Pop I was a model prisoner— what a decent thing to say—and I immediately think The Visions' music is at work in generating that comment. The lecture and punishment I receive are proportionate to the crime, and they work for quite a while.

....

Treachery

It wasn't a pity date. Sofia and I had too good a friendship to label it that. But for our queen to consent to come with me to my senior prom was a special gift. She had graduated from PCHS the year before and developed interests and friendships beyond the boundaries of Plant City. She and I both knew she would be the most beautiful young woman at the event, but though that meant a lot to me, her beauty meant little to her.

Sofia had witnessed first-hand my junior prom in all of its fumbling finesse. She was impressed with the good humor and resilience my date and I had shown when all that could go wrong had. Soon after my junior prom, Sofia agreed to be my date for the senior prom. After I started dating Julie my senior year, I doubted the wisdom of my earlier decision to take Sophia to the prom. But I didn't act on those doubts.

Sofia and her friend at the prom

When first I saw Sofia that night, she was ravishing, in a stately Jackie Kennedy way. She was elegantly tall and slender, radiantly beautiful with big dark hair and an angelic face topping an all-white, long straight dress. Over her dress, she wore a satin cloak with a collar that rose around her slender neck. She could easily have pulled off wearing a crown of jewels.

I helped Sofia into the T-Bird's low-slung, white leather bench seat. As I walked in front of the car to get to my side, I stopped and admired the scene—the pink Thunderbird had never looked so gorgeous, and Sofia matched its beauty and nobly refined style.

The prom was perfect. We danced again for the first time in several months with the same results as in years past: several couples on the dance floor stopped to watch Sofia and what's-his-name move as one in their obvious delight. Whoever Sofia made eye contact with invariably smiled at her in adoration. The music was great, including lots of Motown and British Invasion. We danced to almost every song. We mingled with classmates, some of whom Sofia hadn't seen in a year. We laughed and carried on in our practiced way of being in the moment with a forever friend.

Me in 1965

The meal was excellent, and nothing was spilled all evening. The prom ended too soon. Sofia had to get home, because she was getting up early the next day to leave town. We talked about when she would next be in town and made plans to see each other and others in our group of friends when she returned.

I stopped the car in her driveway and put my arm around her. She looked amused. Then I grabbed her, pulled her to me, and tried to insert my tongue in her mouth.

She pushed me back forcibly, let out a small mournful whimper, and choked out in a whisper, "James, why did you do that?" She opened the car door, turned to face me and, between sobs, said, "Go home, James." I did.

It was the last time I was ever alone with Sofia. We never danced together again. In an instant, my evening with her had gone from exalted euphoria to abject shame. I had betrayed my queen and dearest of friends.

Until those last moments in the T-Bird, I played the role of Sofia's courtier and protecting friend. My crazy, stupid (let's add wrong) behavior was a betrayal of our friendship, and I forfeited all the trust she held in me. I immediately regretted it. I still cherish our earlier friendship, if not the ending of our prom night.

Phate (PO_4^{3-})

Hoppers

Hopper cars full of phosphates from the nearby mines and chemical plants in Bone Valley dominated the freight rail traffic of Plant City throughout my childhood. Some of my earliest memories are of waiting at a railroad crossing in my family's car watching 60 to 80 "phosphate wagons" pass. Some of the wagons carried wet rock phosphate in open hoppers, from the mine sites and their initial processing plants (where the sand, clay, and phosphate were separated) on their way to local chemical processing plants. Others held chemically finished dry rock phosphate in covered hoppers heading to the port of Tampa for transit across the country and planet. Eight phosphate trains a day passed through town, each motored by at least three diesel engines. I saw hundreds of hoppers in a week, each carrying up to 100 tons of "phate."

Bone Valley gets its name from the large deposits of phosphate, fossilized bone fragments, and organic remains in the sand of central Florida. Most of the phosphate mined and manufactured in the valley was used in the production of fertilizer.

The plant at Coronet processed phosphate rock to make alpha tricalcium phosphate, which was used in nutritional supplements for poultry, turkey, cattle, and swine. Sixty-five percent of the nation's phosphate is mined in Bone Valley, which stretches across Polk County and portions of East Hillsborough, Manatee, and Hardee Counties.

My sister and I played train-waiting games while a train full of hoppers passed our folks' car stuck at a railroad crossing. We began with each guessing the number of hoppers—engines and cabooses didn't count—but that was an insufficient challenge to Judy.

We advanced to "three numbers" as the train rolled by. We each said three different numbers out loud, and then watched the cars pass to see if those three numbers appeared in the same order on the side of a hopper. If the last two numbers matched the last two of our three-digit choice, we celebrated a bit. There were no prizes to the winner, but there was a competitive element to the game. When either of us was lucky—right on three consecutive numbers (once or twice a month)—we momentarily forgot we didn't like each other much and laughed in celebration; in the front seat, our parents cheered and applauded our victory, regardless of who "won."

The very rare image of Judy and Jim laughing together at an early age (but no touching)

Mono

....

Sunshine, flowers, darkness. Sunshine, flowers, up in the air, darkness. Sunshine, flowers, still up in the air, people in white moving about, darkness. I wake up fully around sundown. I am in a strange place and can see from the window I'm on the second floor. There are flowers all around the room—vases of daisies and roses, a huge arrangement of bird-of-paradise, chrysanthemums next to my bed, and summer lilies against the window on a stand.

I have a tube in my arm. I close my eyes and drift back into slumber. I wake again. I'm hot, and my throat is sore. A woman in white walks in and stands next to the bed, handing me a cup of water with ice floating around the straw. I sip it slowly and thrill at the feeling in my throat. She smiles, and I smile back.

She says, "Well James, welcome back." I don't remember going anywhere or when I was last someplace. I squeak out a "Hi," which hurts. She smiles again. "Are you up to visitors?" she asks. I nod, which makes my head hurt. She leaves, and Mama and Pop come back with her. They, too, are beaming. They'll kiss me first, I think. But no, they stand at the end of the bed. Seeing my disappointment, Pop explains, "James, you have mononucleosis, and it's contagious. We've been told not to kiss you."

I get out, "Oh. Where am I?"

"We're at South Baptist Hospital. You've been out for 30 hours," Mama tells me.

"What happened?"

Before she can answer, Dr. Weeks comes in, looking happy. He greets my parents and winks at me, then sticks a thermometer in my mouth and starts explaining what's wrong with me. He tells us that it's "mono," a virus, and that the symptoms are fatigue, fever, headaches, swollen lymph nodes in the throat and arm pits, and sore throat. I use my tubeless left arm and hand to feel my throat—yep, there are definite lumps on my jawline, just below both ears.

Dr. Weeks removes the thermometer and asks how many hours I had worked at Coronet earlier that week. I have no idea and reply, "I'm not sure, Doctor Weeks, but I do remember the last part of that day." It starts coming back: "We were re-bricking the giant kiln. Those bricks were heavy and shaped awkwardly—hard to lift and harder to hold. It was hot outside and even hotter inside the oven. They wouldn't let me work more than 20 minutes at a time."

The group nods, and I tell them I'm tired. They wave as they leave.

....

Mines

I worked in the mines several years in a row, beginning with my junior year. The first summer, I was hired by Coronet Industries, Inc., a division of Borden Chemical, at its 2500-acre phosphate chemical processing site three-and-a-half miles southeast of Plant City. I started as a laborer and was assigned to a variety of tasks, ranging from digging trenches to assisting the journeymen running machines and manufacturing gear in the plant. It was hard work.

After recovering from mono, I was transferred to the electrical shop. I carried tools for the electrical journeymen and replaced light bulbs around the plant, which meant standing on ladders—but no heavy lifting. I seldom broke a sweat.

Phosphate plant, Coronet, Florida. 195-?
Black and white photoprint, 8 x 10 in.
State Archives of Florida, Florida Memory.

I worked in the electrical shop again during Christmas break my senior year. I got a pay raise to $1.80 per hour. I always had money in pocket and worked hard at saving nothing.

Upon graduation from high school, I was rehired by Borden Chemical at its Tenoroc (Coronet spelled backwards) mine site. My job was 40 feet up. Four huge drain bins sat beside the first-stage phosphate ore processing plant. The slushy mix made its way up to the top of the bins from the plant by way of a covered conveyor belt that included a catwalk along its side that I used to get atop the bins.

My job was to move the conveyer belt on top of the bins to the next empty bin as the old bin reached capacity. The bins held hundreds of cubic yards of wet phosphate rock and allowed all but 20 percent of the water to drain from the rock. Once the bins had drained sufficiently, the still damp rock was dumped into hopper cars placed under the bins.

 A metal shack on the bin's upper frame kept me out of the elements. It had a heater, AM radio, light, water faucet, urinal of sorts, and cushioned chair. I had to leave the shack to get to the control panel between the bins to move the conveyor belt from one bin to another. It took several hours to fill a bin—I changed bins two or three times a shift.

I worked all three shifts but preferred the graveyard shift. Nights on top of the drying bins were wonderfully peaceful. Tenoroc was eight miles northeast of Lakeland and three miles south of Interstate 4. The lights from the city were far enough away that the darkness beyond the plant sat like a hood on the horizon. The only lights beyond the plant came from the dragline digging site over a half-mile distant.

The wet rock processing plant was noisy, but my station was far enough away that it was more like white noise. If the wind blew favorably, I could hear the sounds of the night from crickets, frogs, chuck-will's-widow, and barred owls. The songbirds began at first light, and their chorus built until sunrise.

A warning mechanism set off a screaming alarm if the bin was about to overflow. On only two occasions over two summers did I miss the alarm and cause a tremendous mess. The second time, the conveyor belts climbing to the bins got so backed up, the entire plant shut down.

I woke with a start, the bin alarm blaring. The alarms started in the section of the plant closest to my station, advancing through the production line to another set of alarms and brilliantly flashing lights. The alarms going off all across the facility were violently loud. I saw my foreman climb the catwalk along the covered conveyor belt leading to me and the drying bin. He had two shovels.

The conveyor belt I controlled over the closest bin was overloaded with wet rock and had been buried in the muck—it was totally frozen up. It took my foreman and me a half hour to dig out the wet phosphate from the end of the belt. When we finished, I moved the belt to the next empty bin. The entire plant was shut down during the incident. After it came back on line and the alarms and flashing lights ceased, my foreman told me to report to him at the end of the shift.

When I met him later, he told me I was being given a warning but would not be fired. He said he expected me to learn from my mistake. Several guys in the plant ribbed me about that night, but not for long. Someone else caused a similar shutdown twice in the same shift a week later, which took the heat off of me. I learned from that and had no other incident on drying bin duty.

My last stint at Tenoroc, in the summer of 1967, was as a dragline oiler, which involved lubricating the moving parts of the dragline, changing minor parts as needed, and performing routine machinery maintenance. A large van could easily fit in the dragline's jaws. The dragline could lift over 50 cubic yards of soil in a single scoop.

My other principal responsibility was moving the eight-inch circumference electrical cable away from the dragline whenever the massive digging machine was moved. Early one night, as our three-man crew was digging phosphate, we were ordered to move the dragline well back from the edge of the pit. We knew a tropical storm was aimed toward south Florida and were informed via phone by the plant superintendent that the storm had picked up speed and was heading for the Lakeland area, with winds expected to exceed 50 miles per hour.

We began the slow, arduous task immediately. The dragline moved on two pontoons, one on each side. The pontoons were raised and moved forward or back over several minutes. The dragline itself was then raised to follow the pontoons to the new location, moving about 20 feet per cycle and taking at least half an hour to move that distance.

My job was performed with the aid of a wooden pole with a metal hook on the working end to snag the 7200 volt, rubber-insulated electric cable going into the back of the dragline—difficult under the best conditions. I had to drag the cable out of harm's way while the dragline was raised on the pontoons.

The only communication I had with the dragline operator was via an industrial switch that hung from the back of the dragline near the cable entry into the dragline. It had two

224

buttons: green for "go" and red for "stop." When I pressed stop, the operator stopped the move of the dragline and awaited my command to continue.

The weather that night got worse by the hour. The dragline operator had requested extra help from the plant. It had been raining for two hours, and I was working in puddles of water that were getting deeper by the minute. I had on heavy rain gear and frequently lost my footing, but using the hook as a cane, I caught myself.

The cable seemed to get heavier as the intensity of the rain and wind increased. We had another 40 feet to back up before we could lower the crane holding the bucket. I fell under the edge of the dragline as it was being lowered onto the pontoons but managed to scramble up and push the red button. It took several minutes to resume the move.

The relief column from the plant arrived soon after my hard fall in the muck. Two guys with their own hooks were assigned to help me move the cable, and, between the three of us, we made significant progress. Although the weather continued to deteriorate, as I saw the crane begin to lower, I knew we had relocated the dragline far enough from the pit for it to be safe. We closed down the dragline, which took a few minutes, and turned off its juice. I looked back from the bed of the pickup on our way to the plant. The seemingly sleeping hulk of the dragline was framed, and even in the gloom of the rain, wind, and dark, it looked quite safe—as was I.

Two Wiah Cawedge

Coach Judy

I heard Gordon's Phys Ed Coach Judy say dozens of times, "If 'ou gonna go to a fowa wiah cawedge, 'ou gotta buckah down." Although he said it much as Tweety Bird might have, his body-builder physique and gymnast athleticism added force to his entreaty. We cadets chuckled softly at his high-pitched, speech-impeded mantra about "buckling down."

He was an enchanting contradiction with his masculine physique and feminine name, his booming but high-pitched voice, and his baby-talk speech. He could press hundreds of pounds of steel but was incapable of lifting his tongue to articulate the l, r, and y sounds. He was also quite right. Many cadets took his counsel to heart. I ignored it thoroughly.

Coach Judy on a trampoline

(In the news of Southeast Asia, 1965 had started with a contingent of approximately 23,000 American troops in Vietnam. The first march against the war in D.C. that April had 20,000 protesters. By July, American troops numbered

125,000 and the draft was expanded from 17,000 to 35,000 a month. In September, *Washington Post* columnist Joseph Alsop wrote the war had reached "the light at the end of the tunnel." At year's end, there were 184,000 American troops in Vietnam. In 1965, the number of U.S. fatalities rose from 216 in 1964 to 1,928.)

Freshman

My grandfather, Roy, would pay for my college, but only if I attended Oral Roberts University or a military college. I never considered Oral Roberts and its evangelical underpinnings. I did considerable research on several two-year military colleges across the country. Gordon Military College in Barnesville, Georgia, was coed—well, there you go. It offered a high school program for local students—including a large number of females. The 450-person junior college also had several female students, none serving as military cadets. I could not imagine going to college with an all-male student body. I declared my decision, and Roy agreed.

A segment of boys at Gordon had found their way to Barnesville with little real choice, due mostly to bad grades in school or behavior problems. A few had been offered attendance at Gordon as an alternative to reform school by juvenile courts across the south. The majority of my classmates were good guys looking for fun when they could find it, but several cadets consistently looked for trouble. They helped balance out several other cadets who were disturbingly gung-ho.

Most of us (including all of my friends) complained constantly about life at Gordon and viewed the military training as regrettably necessary crap. It was acceptable to "play the game," but being zealous was widely viewed with contempt.

The college was located ten miles west of Interstate 75, approximately halfway between Atlanta and Macon, Georgia. The tuition rates were relatively low compared with other boarding schools and therefore attracted numerous Latin American and Puerto Rican boys—but no blacks.

The uniforms—cotton in summer and wool in winter— were Rebel gray. We had to wear grey hats whenever we were in uniform and outside.

The Confederate Stars and Bars could be seen around campus on dorm and barracks entrances, in windows, and at all sporting events. The junior college was a football prep school, dressing out 100 players. A quarter of the cadets were football players. I tried out but lost interest. There were football games at the campus stadium both weekend nights—Friday for high school and Saturday for college.

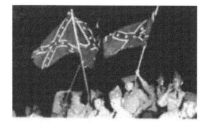

Gordon cadets cheering at a home football game

My first week as a plebe/cadet was intended to test me. It was challenging, but seeing other boys deal with the hazing more poorly than I somehow gave me strength, if not pleasure. The hazing began immediately for my new roommate and me. Mike and I were forced to stand at attention outside our room while half a dozen senior cadets ripped our bedding apart, threw trash cans down the hall, trashed our clothes, yelled at us, made us do push-ups, and kept us at attention for a couple of hours at a time.

It was unpleasant, but no one was injured, although most of us were embarrassed, physically exhausted, intimidated, angry, and questioning our decision to go to military school.

The institutional hazing was interrupted in late September by an outbreak of crabs that resulted in the entire cadet corps being marched to communal showers and stripped, with both hands holding a towel over our heads while we were sprayed with bellows by men in latex gear. It looked as if the entire brigade had nakedly surrendered to the men in the rubber suits as we waited in line to be doused with a white powder composed of DDT and talcum. The crabs were thoroughly massacred.

Soon after the crabs incident, an assembly was held in the Gordon gym that was attended by all of the cadets and hundreds of townsfolk to learn how to use the new rotary telephones that had finally made their way to Barnesville. Mike and I felt like we were stepping back into the 1940s as the instruction continued. We had rotary phones as far back as we could recall in our hometowns of Charleston and Plant City. Prior to the rollout of the new equipment, if you wanted to place a call, you picked up the receiver and "Betsy" would come on the line saying, "number please." We cadets thought the current phone system and the assembly presentation were on the "backward" side of "quaint" and confirmed to Mike and me that we were living in the boonies.

A routine was established quickly of reveille at 6:30 a.m. (a piped-in bugle call), assembly formation in front of the administration building for roll call, the raising of the flag, and the firing of the cannon. We marched to breakfast and then back to the dorm to prepare for classes starting at 8.

Sunday's reveille was an hour later than other days. After assembly, we had breakfast. Around 8:30, we formed into two units—Baptist and Methodist. The first service was composed exclusively of cadets. A second service for the townspeople followed. After church, we marched the 12 blocks back to campus. I hated marching to and from church.

After the second week, I checked around and discovered that a Catholic service was held at 11:30 at a small building directly across the street from the college and cadets just walked to the service. I became Catholic for the next two years. But I didn't take communion.

I slept as late as I wanted, skipped breakfast, went to church, and had a large, leisurely lunch as my meal of the day. I liked the priest, and the small congregation of a few cadets and a dozen or so townies made the service much more accessible and meaningful to me; and I learned to appreciate the church's sacraments.

(In Vietnam news, Chet Huntley and David Brinkley of NBC reported in March 1966 the South Vietnamese cities of Hue and Da Nang experienced large uprisings by Buddhist anti-government, anti-American demonstrators. In June, the U.S. consulate in Hue was stormed. Ex-Vice President Nixon called for 500,000 American troops in Vietnam and for increased bombing of Hanoi in August. 1966 would see 382,000 American men drafted—the most in any year of the Vietnam War.)

Winter quarter, I began to cut my first class, Phys Ed, regularly so that after assembly and breakfast, I could return to the barracks for uninterrupted sleep. By the end of the quarter, I began cutting ROTC out of lack of interest.

With football season over, the college held weekend dances at a recreation hall across from campus. Music was pervasive on campus. We all had radios tuned to our favorite music stations. The canteen in the basement of the barracks next to Watson Hall had a fine jukebox.

Stereo players could be heard in numerous rooms in the barracks playing albums ranging from the Beatles, the Kinks, and the Stones to Johnny Cash and Hank Williams. You could hear Bob Dylan, the Supremes, James Brown, Otis Redding, and Miles Davis in a short walk down the hall, but there was no dancing there.

My first dance was with a high school girl who quickly picked up my best funky moves, and we owned the dance hall that first night. She was from Atlanta, visiting a girlfriend in Barnesville—never saw her again. That dip in the girl-pool of flowing movement captured me completely.

I was a regular at the weekend dances for the rest of the school year. None of my encounters led to a date, but I was thrilled to be around girls again. I enjoyed the conversations as much as the dancing, but the dancing kept me coming back.

By the end of the second quarter, the discipline in the barracks lightened up. What had been daily inspections of the room now only occurred on Saturdays. We still had to fold and place our underwear, undershirts, and socks in a set order in our small closets and hang our uniforms in a prescribed manner. Our two pairs of shoes were spit-polished. The cement floors had to be mopped repeatedly to a fine and spotless shine, the sink and mirror squeaky clean, and the trash can immaculate. Our bunks were made with hospital corners, with the top wool blanket pulled stiff enough to bounce a quarter on top.

I lost most of my money at poker games in the barracks. My $8 a week spending allowance from home was quickly in jeopardy, so I went into the sock business. I had a charge account at Wisebram's Department Store in downtown Barnesville for incidentals. Every cadet had to wear black socks daily, and most of us had at least ten pairs.

 I could buy a stock of socks at a quarter a pair and sell them on campus for 20¢, saving my numerous customers a nickel per pair of socks and helping them avoid the mile walk into town. Every pair of socks I sold was pure profit— I was clearing about $10 per month—and my parents didn't complain about the charges until the end of the school year, when they promptly closed the account.

Accomplice

During the winter quarter, I had made friends with several guys who had cars on campus, and we began to visit nearby towns where there were movie theaters and a wider selection of girls—and fewer guys. I had become a world-class wing man in high school.

My three-year older friend Gene was a popular local rock and roll lead singer and was successful with girls. I introduced Gene to several of my female high school classmates, and he dated three or four of them off and on. I was accomplished at supporting Gene's best moves— which took little work; in fact, the more I relaxed, the better I could buttress his efforts and look for a girl of my own.

Early in spring quarter, Lt. Blood, our Company Commander, and I, along with my swellest-of-fellows roommate, Mike, decided to go to Griffin, Georgia, to pick up some dates. We stopped at a drive-in restaurant for burgers and learned there was a high school dance a few blocks away.

We were in our civvies and soon realized we were the coolest guys in the gym. I did my dance thing while Blood worked the small pockets of girls around the gym, and Mike followed Blood's example. After a few songs, we left with three cute young girls. No more than three blocks from the school, we were pulled over by two very unhappy Spalding County deputies.

After installing the girls in the back of the squad car, the deputies told us to follow them to the county jail. Talking about our situation on the way, we agreed we had not done anything wrong and would soon be free to go. We were so wrong.

We were quickly informed that one of the girls was 15 and the daughter of the county sheriff. We were fingerprinted and locked up to await the sheriff's arrival. Two deputies brought in our half-drunk bottle of Rebel Yell bourbon and the remains of two six packs of Pabst Blue Ribbon beer. These two officers also looked most unhappy.

It took the sheriff about an hour to show up—we suspected he was busy delivering a memorable lecture to his daughter on the dangers of boys from Gordon. He studied us silently for a couple of minutes.

His first words were, "Your parents or your commandant?" I immediately said, "Commandant, please sir."

Spalding County took every penny we had. Major Dickinson, our commandant whom we had awakened, agreed that we would be released into his custody and no charges would be filed, but that Gordon would punish us acutely. It was a quiet ride back to campus.

Lt. Blood wasn't busted, but he got twice as many demerits and hours marching around the quadrant as Mike and I got—30 hours with a rifle at present arms. Mike and I lost our stripes. The recurring theme of the major's repeated ass-chewing was that we were unlucky and stupid. Even in private, we agreed. We didn't return to Griffin.

1966 Delta Company, 3rd Platoon
(me, last row 2nd from left, Mike, first row, 4th from right)

I finished the year with a low C average, failing both Phys Ed and ROTC. I pulled a B in history and English. I managed to gain back a stripe the last quarter and worked off all of my demerits. I looked forward to summer back home in Plant City and my return to the phosphate plant. I didn't dread returning to Gordon.

Gordon Not

Gordon Military College was not for everyone. About 30 percent of those attending as freshmen did not return. Gordon was generally not pleasant. There was incessant ironing of shirts and pants until crinkly stiff. We had to "pop to" by standing at attention with our backs pressed against the wall when an officer passed us in the hall. Arbitrary group punishment awaited an entire barracks when a single cadet screwed up badly.

Each week night, we had an enforced study time of two hours. Occasional violence erupted when a particularly brutish officer or hard-ass noncommissioned officer went too far and suffered a blanket party; the officer was ambushed, a blanket thrown over his head so he couldn't identify his attackers, held down, and pummeled by fists. However, Gordon was also not without its delightful moments and experiences.

Raising the colors

(In April 1967, Muhammad Ali refused to be inducted into the armed forces, based on conscientious objector status.

He brashly proclaimed, "I ain't got no quarrel with them Viet Cong.")

Sophomore

My roommate Mike and I moved to the second floor of Watson Hall at the beginning of our second year at Gordon. We were allowed more privileges, including the purchase of a small cheap cotton rug and a cheaper end table that made a fine card table. We were both promoted to sergeant that quarter. (I would lose all my stripes for the second time later that year for various infractions, misdemeanors, and mischief.)

We made a new set of friends, in addition to the guys we knew from the previous year. The fall of 1966 saw a large reduction in the amount of hazing that had been practiced by the brigade. We were relieved that we wouldn't have to torture the new cadets. The first black high school cadet was admitted that quarter—apparently without incident. My grades hovered around C, except for Phys Ed and ROTC, which I consistently failed due to poor attendance.

Repeat

Sgt. Rich was a petite guy with angular features who resembled a young Wally Cox. He had a speech tic that was fascinating. Whatever he said, I mean *whatever* he said, he repeated, you know, said it twice. Not everyone noticed it, some didn't. Once you did, after noticing it, you couldn't un-notice it, it was impossible to ignore. It was weird, you know, strange. It was entertaining, kind of fun. He had three stripes, being a sergeant. He led our platoon;

he was in charge of our first formation in the morning, early a.m.

One day, a weekday, we fell in properly and Rich took his position in front of the 35 cadets under his command. He ordered, "Attention." From the back of the ranks, Lumpy said softly, "Attention," as the platoon came to attention. Rich's command did not require repeating, and Lumpy had broken protocol by his act. Several of us snickered. Rich didn't address Lumpy's insubordination. He called out, "Left face." Three or four voices in unison and in a hushed tone responded, "Left face," as the platoon performed the maneuver. There were several chuckles from the cadets.

Rich called out, "Forward, march!" and the entire platoon responded, again softly, "Forward, march." Rich became flustered; I'm sure the laughter didn't help. He turned suddenly and walked back to the barracks. It was rather sad, and later, when our cadet commander, Lt. Blood, called us together, he applied a proper reprimand. We had to individually apologize to Sgt. Rich—which seemed redundant. We were issued two demerits each (that's twice one) and grounded for a weekend—you know, we could not leave the barracks except for meals.

Sally

I met Sally early in September of that year. I had noticed her before—although only a sophomore in high school, she was the most sensual girl on campus, with long, blond hair and a disarming smile, and she moved with girlish ease. My first encounter with her was at a dance on a weekend when both the college and high school football teams had away games.

Soon after the doors opened, I asked her to dance. She laughed through the entire song, and her carefree romp was spellbinding. She asked me to dance with her for a second record. We didn't ask after that, we just kept dancing. The rec hall lights flashed on and off too quickly that night, and we said goodbye, sharing a small hug.

I saw Sally several times the following week as we randomly passed each other on our way to class. We spoke briefly each time and at some length one day in the canteen. She told me there was a county fair in Spalding County the upcoming weekend and that she'd like me to join her and another couple on Sunday afternoon. She was clear in letting me know it wasn't a date. We both laughed when I wrote out a note to her that read, "I will go, I will behave, and it won't be a date in any way." I gave her the note, and she folded it carefully and placed in her pocket.

Mike (far left) chatting up the coeds at the canteen in front of the rockin' juke box

Major Bear

It was a gorgeous afternoon. Sally's friends Virginia and Tim, would pick us up at Sally's house. I walked the half mile to her home (a very comfortable brick house) and met her mother, whom I took to immediately. Sally was dressed in a turquoise blue sweater and white pleated skirt—she was striking. The dating couple and nondating couple (Jim and Sally) arrived at the fair and went directly to the midway. We ate carnival snacks and rode rides to lots of laughter and screaming. Sally and I checked out the games of chance/skill as Virginia and Tim rode more rides.

At the milk bottle booth, Sally began jumping up and down when she spotted the large stuffed bear offered as a prize to anyone who could knock down all three bottles stacked on top of each other. I had my doubts, but the carny running the game begged me to try.

I gave him a quarter and threw the very squishy softball at the bottom of the pyramid where the bottles intersect—as suggested by the carny. He also told me to throw hard, but not to overthrow. It was as if he was helping me win. After one throw, I did.

The carny removed the giant teddy from its perch and handed it to Sally with some difficulty. She kissed it with surprising passion. The carny looked almost as happy as Sally—the bear, too, seemed mildly amused. It was a happy moment, equal to any I had had at Gordon.

The carny told the two of us that he would appreciate our help by sending anyone who asked about Major Bear— that's what Sally had named it—his way. I knew then the carny did want me to win that bear and had helped make that happen. Having a pretty, young girl win and then work the crowd was brilliant marketing.

She insisted on carrying Major Bear herself and, when asked where she won it, raised Major's huge paw and pointed to the booth or acted as if the bear was giving directions in a raspy voice, "By that Ferris wheel over there," again pointing with the paw. I have no doubt the carny had a profitable day, given the number of folks we encouraged to try their luck with his milk bottles.

What had been planned for a two-hour visit was going on four hours. Virginia finally insisted we leave. Sally and I carried Major to the car together. We didn't kiss on that first date.

Wooing

A few weeks later, Sally and I met at the rec hall for more dancing. We held hands between songs. After the dance ended, Sally suggested I join her, Virginia, and Tim for a milk shake at the Dairy Queen. Sally and I climbed in the back seat of Tim's car and immediately started making out. I can't say who initiated that first kiss, so let's call it a tie.

There were numerous extended clinches, a few sighs from Sally, and a groan or two from me. I thought I was the luckiest guy in the brigade and was thoroughly surprised by my advancement from wing man to solo pilot. I couldn't quite believe I was dating Sally and that she might consent to be my girlfriend.

Sally and I continued to date and were beginning to fall in love. I was always thankful to her for being with me and for opening up her home to me. We were discreet. I was determined to be a gentleman and fully respected the limits she placed on our petting. It was a lovely, young romance.

Plant City Rendezvous

We made plans to go to Plant City for spring break to introduce Sally to my family and enjoy the Florida beach. Both of our families approved of our plans, and we set off with two Gordon cadets headed to Jacksonville, Florida. They dropped us off at a Howard Johnson's restaurant, where I called my parents to beg them to pick us up for the rest of trip. My parents, amazingly, agreed and drove the 200 miles to pick us up (and of course 200 miles back home).

In Plant City, Sally stayed with my grandparents Foster. She loved their house. They made her comfortable, and they were charmed by her. I stayed with my parents on Johnson Street. Mom Foster dropped Sally off at our house mid-morning our first full day in town. We had been invited to our neighbor Arnie's house for an afternoon in his swimming pool.

He was a 60-something cattleman, sportsman, and one of Pop's best bass fishing buddies. I discovered that bikini-clad colleens were also his quarry. He served us Cokes and snacks and ogled Sally. It became uncomfortable for Sally, and I got angry and showed it. He took the hint and left us alone. He invited us back, but I didn't say yes.

Smashing Cars

Pop loaned me his pink '57 Thunderbird for our date that night. I had mixed results with that car when it came to dating but I knew Sally would be thrilled to ride in it. We planned to go up State Road 38 and U.S. Highway 301 to a dance in Dade City. We got a late start.

We stopped at a Spur station just south of Dade City for me to buy some cigarettes. I left Sally in the car after parking in a space beside the station.

When I returned, I started the engine, slipped it into drive, and hit the accelerator—hard enough to hear the engine sing. There was an immediate violent lurch, and the car bounced backward. I had hit something. Hard. Sally had been jerked forward with force. I asked if she was okay and she said, "Yes. What was that?" I got out and saw a dent in the driver's side front steel wheel and matching dent in the passenger's side front wheel—about one-half inch deep. I had parked in front of a 12" cement curb that someone must have been placed there while I was inside the station.

We needed to go back to Plant City. It was after 10 p.m., and I didn't want to take any chances with the T-Bird. The car was very wobbly, so I drove slowly. About five miles north of Zephyrhills, the right front tire blew. Before I could get off the road, the left tire blew. I knew this was real trouble, because auto makers foolishly limit the number of spare tires to one.

We were in a shallow valley in the dark, except for a couple of lights a quarter mile away in what looked like a barn. When no one stopped to help after an hour, we agreed I should walk to the barn and ask to use the phone. Turns out, the barn was part of a dairy farm and the two men running the operation were busy setting up their milking machines. It was very loud, but I finally got one man's attention. He apologized, saying there was no phone.

I returned to Sally and decided to drive the last few miles into Zephyrhills, at a crawl, to call Pop for help. It was approaching 5 a.m., and it was still dark by the time we found a pay phone. He was angry and sleepy when he picked us up. He was worried about his car but was more concerned that we were okay.

We slept most of the day. That night, we picked up Trey and his girlfriend to see a drive-in movie in Lakeland. The T-Bird was shot, so I borrowed my mother's car. The line of cars going into the drive-in was formidable. I noticed that there was no line in the other direction, so I continued past the entrance to make a u-turn at the first break in the median, but the car just wouldn't turn far enough.

We watched as a single headlight approached down the road toward us. I was stuck in middle of the road. Traffic behind me wouldn't allow me to back up, and in front of me was a ditch. I tried backing up a little and turning the wheel hard to straighten out. My mother's car and the one-eyed object began sharing the same space. I was thankful it was a ragged pickup truck and not a motorcycle.

No one was hurt, but my mother's car had taken a hit on the back right fender. The truck had almost skidded to a complete stop before hitting us and suffered minor damage. We skipped the movie and went home.

My family was out of cars, and my grandparents didn't offer—to their obvious credit. My best friend, Gene, though, insisted I take his classic 1955 Ford to Clearwater Beach the next day to show Sally the best of Florida beaches. We had a wonderful time at the beach and lingered for hours. I was sure Sally was the most beautiful girl on the beach and I the envy of many.

Driving home through downtown Clearwater, Gene's car suddenly made a loud crashing noise as I ran a red light. Let's talk about that red light. Later, a cop would tell me there was only one light in Pinellas County that did not hang in the middle of the intersection. It was on this street corner. Most unfair.

I had wiped out the entire driver's side of a brand new Oldsmobile Tornado driven by a 16-year old with her grandmother as a passenger. Sally went to the hospital with contusions, and I went to jail.

I had wrecked four cars in under a week, if you include the Oldsmobile (the one-eyed pickup truck was dented some, but including it would be bragging). Sally was distressed, Pop was pissed, but my mother really wasn't angry, because she felt guilty about not telling me the power steering had gone out in her car prior to my accident. Trey was amused. Gene was really pissed.

Pop bailed me out. Sally and I went back to Barnesville on a Greyhound bus. It was a long, mostly silent ride, but we did sit together. We had created some memories that stuck. Later that year, there were pledges of love and talk of marriage.

(Early in my last quarter at Gordon, reports started coming in that Gordon graduates and alumni had been killed in Southeast Asia. The war had become personal. The 1967 news from Vietnam reported 485,000 U.S. troops in that country, with 11,153 killed in action.)

Parting

Sally and I went to Paradise Beach at Lanier Island for a day late in the spring—again, Sally was the prettiest girl there. In a quiet moment, looking at guys looking at Sally, I knew I could not possibly maintain our relationship from a distance—but I didn't express that reality to her or admit it to myself.

I found it difficult to accept that our relationship was ending and acted in a way that insured it did. It ended sloppily and poorly, through no fault of Sally's. I said words that shouldn't have been said and wrote letters with sentiments best not expressed. Sadly, my last letter to her ended the possibility of further communication.

I was miserable about having lost Sally, and parts of myself, in my jealous passion. I destroyed our relationship by my possessive longings. I was glad to leave Barnesville. It was not a place where I excelled. Was that the fault of Sally, the people I met there, or Gordon? No, it was not.

Part Seven – Groan-up

Coastin' Part 1 – Jersey and Philly

I applied to the University of South Florida in Tampa, went to few classes, and then found myself back at the phosphate mine as a dragline oiler. I earned high wages, enjoyed going out, and got too inebriated almost nightly. Having lost my college deferment to the draft and having no desire to work at the mine or visit Vietnam, I volunteered for military service. I couldn't get into the Navy or Army Reserves. I joined the U.S. Coast Guard.

Pop was a Coastie in the 1940s, Uncle Bobby in the '50s, and me in the '60s. We were all honorably discharged. None of us got shot while serving, and I was only shot at once. I reported to boot camp in early December 1967 in Cape May, New Jersey—a seaside resort town at the southern tip of the Garden State. It was cold, the days were short, and the weather was usually nasty.

The Helms Coasties (me, Pop, Uncle Bobby)

Boot Camp

The first weeks were harsh but not brutal. It was only a little worse than my early plebe weeks my first year at Gordon. Our drill instructor, Chief Richie, made us all miserable, and we thought him sadistic. Our first week of boot camp, a cold front hit with gale-force winds and freezing rain with temperatures in the low 20s. Several windows on our new third-floor home couldn't be closed. The wind blew through our bunks, so many recruits slept in their clothes. Additional blankets were issued, and we could hear Chief Richie raise hell in the barracks latrine with his superior officer about the windows. It cheered us to know he had our backs and our cold fronts. The windows were fixed the next day.

Me in my official U. S. Coast Guard "duck hat"

I made friends quickly with several fellow sufferers. James, an African American reservist from New York City, was witty, good-natured, and hard-working. I had never had a conversation with a black male my own age until boot camp. We hit it off. Having a biracial friendship was special to me, and he clearly thought me a good guy. I also became friends with Don from Massachusetts and found him to be cheerful and thoughtful. He and I aced a standardized aptitude test and were assigned to aviation electronics training at the U.S. Naval Training Station in Millington, Tennessee, a few miles north of Memphis. We were to report in March 1968.

Our boot camp company (me, front row, on left with holster)

Ping, Ping

I got leave in February to visit Plant City for almost a week. My buddy, Trey, and I got dates and went out on the town. Later, we all went to my grandparents Fosters' house for an after-party. I knew my grandparents were traveling for the whole winter and the four of us would have the run of the large house. I had pocketed the key to their house from a bowl at my house. I had no problem opening the double garage door. There was a strange car next to my grandmother's, but I thought nothing of it.

We were all high on beer and being loud. What of it? Trey and I climbed the steps to the back door while our dates waited in the car. We had left the headlights on so we could see what we were doing. I tried the key. It didn't fit. I tried again, with no luck.

A small firecracker went off from the other side of the door. I heard a distinct ping, ping across the garage deck. I didn't know what was happening. I yelled, "Roy, Zola!" Someone from inside the house answered in German. I yelled again, "Roy, it's Jim!" We then heard a voice asking in English, "Who is it?" I answered, "I'm Roy's grandson. Who are you?" The voice replied, "We rented the house."

The lights came on in the kitchen and the garage. The back door opened, and a man with a 22-caliber snub nose revolver in his hand nodded to us. Apologies were expressed in English and regrets in call-it-German. There was also a very neat, round hole in the door, about chest high between where Trey and I had been standing. Everyone wished each other good night, and we decided that it was a fine time to end the evening.

Trip

The Coast Guard was sending Don and I to the center of the United States so we could learn all there was to know about electronics from the Navy and Marines. The Navy having a station in Tennessee didn't seem right, somehow.

We decided to make our transfer to Memphis an exploit, not just a trip. For about $120, we could have flown to Memphis in three hours. Since we had three days to make the journey, we chose instead the promising alternative of a train trip through the heartland. We calculated it would take two days by bus and rail and we could pass through Philly, D.C., Chattanooga, and Nashville.

I had a lifelong romance with trains. My hometown was named for a railroad tycoon. Train whistles and crossing signal bells were the soundtrack of my life from infancy to age 18. I had counted rail phosphate hopper cars as a kid and seen them filled while working at the phosphate mines. I had ridden trains as a tyke to the state fair in Tampa and as a teen across much of the southeast United States. My great uncle worked for the Santa Fe Railroad. I loved trains. Going to Memphis on a train would be a perfect adventure.

Wretched Trailways

....

It is another raw, dull March morning. Don and I have our $5 bus tickets to Philadelphia, Pennsylvania. We are waiting in the shed for the interstate bus to make its scheduled pickup at Cape May. Our olive drab canvas duffel bags are brimming, and we use them as foot rests as we huddle in our pea coats.

The bus, empty except for the driver, pulls up to the shelter. We fumble with our four-foot long bags and stumble to seats in the next-to-last row. We set our duffels next to us on the deck of the bus. We are comfortable, anticipating a peaceful three-hour, 90-mile trip that will end in downtown Philly.

Our private leisure is interrupted by the faint sounds of choking directly behind us. Our impression of having the bus to ourselves is corrected, as the coughing fellow grabs the back of the seat in front of him with both hands and pulls himself up into a lopsided sitting position. We shrug and, with faint smiles, resume our contemplation of the snowy countryside.

Suddenly, there is a deep retch, followed immediately by a definite splash. Our initial shock is compounded by the ongoing sounds of our companion's bucking stomach. The smell of stale wine wafts our way and is soon joined by a variety of underdigested aromas.

I try to open my window, without success. I am surprised when, looking down; I see an oozy puddle making its way to Don's duffel bag. I tap Don on the shoulder and point as the residue encircles his bag. Don immediately yanks the bag into his lap and begins to wipe the bottom with a handkerchief that miraculously appears in his hand.

As I pull my bag into the seat in front of me, I tap Don on the shoulder again and once more point down. The puddle is more a sluggish streamlet now. Don is grappling with the duffel bag in his lap and focusing on getting it clean. I point to his left foot, which is presenting itself as a black polished island in a tide of mysterious flotsam. Don heaves his bag into the seat in front of him as he raises his foot—a very awkward move. The duffel bag's momentum tears it out of his grasp, and it lands with a pronounced splat in the ever-spreading goo.

We move way up front. The driver tells us he can't kick the guy off the bus because he is a "regular passenger and rarely gets this sick." He says the windows have been "winterized" and will not open. His window is open. Don and I share the same bench just behind the driver for the rest of the way to Philly.

Our bags have separate seats. Don's bag needs to be alone for a while. My duffel is quite clean; Don's is rank. When we reach the bus station in Philly, we don't look back at our fellow passenger. We need to wash off Don's shoe and spiff up his reeking duffel bag.

....

The Pirate Strikes

We thought the bus station and the train station were in the same building. We were within three miles of being right. The clerk at the bus station said we could catch a cross-town city bus at the stop two blocks away. We could see a nest of idling buses across the intersection from where we stood. The clerk told us our bus was the B-7.

Don and I were in our dress blue sailor suits. In the Coast Guard, that includes a silly-looking hat like one the British Navy wears, with a wide black band that keeps the Donald Duck hat snugly on your head with the words, "U.S. Coast Guard" across the front.

As we approached the intersection, the pedestrian crossing sign showed a "foot." Suddenly, two matrons grabbed Don's arm and said they wanted to thank him. We were trying to figure out if we had done some charitable act unknown to us that these ladies had observed, or if their thanks were an obscure extension of "brotherly love." All this, while keeping one eye on the bus stop beyond the intersection.

Sure enough, the B-7 was edging its way up the street. The line of buses was four or five deep, and each bus took several minutes to unload and reload. The "foot" sign cycled as the matrons told us we should be proud. We still couldn't figure out why we were being thanked. They asked for our addresses so that they could write to us in Vietnam. Oh . . .

"We are on our way to Tennessee, ladies, and we don't know our address yet," Don was explaining. I wondered if Don was also going to explain we were doing all we could to keep out of Vietnam. I noticed the B-7 had eased by three other waiting buses and was now pulling up to the stop. "Foot" was just changing to "hand" as Don took a pen and paper from the more silver-haired of the two. I guess he was going to give them his folks' address. I started yelling, "It's the B-7, it's the B-7!"

I turned to see Don trying to disengage from our matrons. His bag was slung over his shoulder, and he was backing into the street while writing his address. The drivers in Philly stop for sailors. I was almost to the bus, and there was only one man waiting to get on. I don't know if he was blind, but he had a cane. Back then, buses didn't accommodate the disabled. He couldn't negotiate the step, and Mr. Cute, the driver, was letting off the brake just enough to crawl forward and keep the man off balance.

Don was suddenly behind me. He reached over my back and tapped the man with the cane. As he turned, I darted past him and bolted up the steps. Out of the corner of my eye, I saw a cane fly by the windows. Don leaped on the bus just as Mr. Cute released the B-7 from its berth.

Don had the matron's pen in his mouth. His bag was snagged on the fare box, and he was just getting it loose as Mr. Cute floored it. I had my bag between my knees, settled in a spot near the front door when Don flew by. He made a nifty move and fell into the empty seat on the bench that runs sideways behind the driver. His duffel bag came to rest upright beside him, thanks to gravity and some random laws of physics. Don was smiling like a pirate. The matron's pen, a lovely cloisonné affair, cut his smile like a miniature cutlass.

I then noticed a small, pale hand emerge from behind Don's bag. Looking closer, I saw another spring out from the other side. It looked like Don's bag was trying to liftoff. Both hands, and now tiny arms, were flaying the air much like a giant hummingbird with thin white wings. The effect was hypnotizing.

I noticed all conversation around me had stopped, as if on a bird watch, some of Audubon's best were witnessing a superb display of a rare chick's first flight. That's when the woman screamed, "My baby!" It would have been less alarming and more accurate to have screamed, "My three-year-old toddler!" but "My baby!" worked.

Don and I bumped heads loud enough to hear the thud, even over the hyperventilating child's first wail. Don's yucky duffel bag had completely covered the tyke, and, had it not managed to free its still waving little arms, I guess we would have had a tragedy. The mother thought it was one. I think the kid was never in danger of asphyxiation. Granted, Don's bag was heavy and, given our previous messy bus trip, beyond ripe, but still. I think several more seconds were available to the child.

At a red light, Don spotted our patriotic matrons standing two blocks from where we left them. The bus caught up to them and—remembering the pen in his mouth—the rest was reflex. He took the pen out of his mouth, jumped to the other side of the bus, threw open the window, and hit one of our matrons in the lower back with it. She screamed.

I don't know why Don did that. I guess it had something to do with feeling poorly about almost killing a kid and wanting to return the lady's pen. His fluid, feline move that ended with a direct hit on a dear, sweet, little old lady certainly quieted the aggrieved mom and rapidly reviving child.

At the train station, we learned our two-day trip would take close to 60 hours. We bought our tickets, a mere $50, and caught the train to Union Station in Washington, D.C.

Continued in Coastin' Part 2 – D.C. and Bristol

Coastin' Part 2 — D.C. and Bristol

D.C. but Not So Much A.C.

We got in at dark, stowed our duffel bags in two rental lockers, and got lost.

I don't remember passing any monuments, nor do I think we crossed any bridges. Still, we were in D.C., the drinking age was 18, and we had saved big money by foregoing the airplane.

We walked about 20 blocks and spotted an adult theater with a small bar next door. I don't know if walking under the bright theater marquee ruined our night vision, but the bar was plenty dark. We were inside, though, and Don managed to find two empty bar stools.

We ordered two beers and didn't even get carded. The black barkeep brought us two cold ones, and the first clear vision I had in the bar was of his hands, with lots of rings and very long nails.

I turned and looked into the smoky depths of the place. Most of the crowd was in the rear of the bar. People were slow-dancing to a Johnny Mathis song playing on the juke box, and in the closest booth, a couple was making out.

A gentleman walked up to me from behind and asked a haunting question: "You do know where you are, right boys?" As I turned, I saw him walking out the front door.

I told Don I thought we ought to leave. Don looked at me as if I had just announced my intention to become a bookshelf. He said he was having fun and asked why I wanted to leave. I suggested he look around.

I followed Don's gaze as it swept the bar. His back straightened, noticeably, as he eyed the nearest booth. The two lovers were just finishing their deep kiss as Don made eye contact with one of the guys, who caught the eyes of Guy Two and directed them toward Don.

Both guys looked straight into Don's open face and licked their parted lips, and Guy Two winked. They were friendly, and the bar was mellow, but that wasn't the kind of fun we were looking for.

I was on my feet, pouring the beer down my throat and putting money on the bar at the same time. "Let's go," were my only words.

Don then did something amazing. He started taking baby sips from his glass. I don't mean short swallows. No, it was closer to how you might sip boiling water. I said, "Let's go," and put money on the bar for Don.

He took more baby sips. I repeated, "Let's go," He put his beer down, caught his breath, and took more baby sips. "Let's go!" Baby sips, catch breath, baby sips, "Let's go," baby sips.

I felt like I was stuck in the middle of a long, bad joke. Halfway through his 12-ounce Bud, Don broke the pattern by announcing, "I can't guzzle beer." Baby sips. That's when I reached over, took the beer out of his hand and finished it. Don was pissed and relieved.

We walked more blocks. We heard rock and roll and saw pretty girls dancing on raised platforms. In short skirts. We paid the bouncer $5 each to get into the bar with the go-go girls. There were two of them and two of us when we ordered our $3 beers. There was one of them when we finished our first beer. She brought us our second round and said she was going upstairs to "The Club."

Don and I sat in the empty bar with a bouncer outside and wondered if our uniforms were the reason we were abandoned. We also wondered how we were going to get more beer.

We asked the bouncer about The Club. He told us for $5 each we could join. We bought one-year memberships.

The Club was up a wide flight of stairs, down a poorly lit hall. Inside, there were flashing lights. The room was large, but dozens of people were dancing on the tiny dance floor about the size of a floor furnace grill. The go-go girls were now in cages six feet off the deck. Although we saw several women, none of them would talk to us or accept our offers for a beer or a dance.

Don and I agreed later that it was definitely the uniforms' fault. As we finished our beers and made our way to the street, we noticed the same two girls were back in the small bar dancing for three guys. We started back but were stopped by our bouncer buddy and club sponsor. He told us that would be another $5. Don explained we had a membership. No good. Don explained we had already paid $5 to get in the small bar originally. No good.

We got directions to Union Station. They were no good.

At 3 a.m., we found Union Station. Our train, the Tennessean, left for Chattanooga at 8 a.m. We would be on the home stretch once in Nooga. I was familiar enough with Tennessee and looked forward to the Tennessean taking us through Nooga and Nashville. We slept on benches until 6 a.m., when the morning rush hour began. Sleep ended with a jolt as 20 small children speaking a Scandinavian tongue that mostly involved screeching vowel sounds cleared the building of all insects and lower-order rodents.

Jesus in a Bag

We boarded the train in a crowd. We had a choice of but two seats. One was next to a rather large young man with bad skin, holding a huge, bulging briefcase to his chest. The other was several rows back, next to the female half of a proper-looking elderly couple who had taken seats facing one another. She had on a charming lavender outfit topped with a dainty, matching pill box hat. Don beat me to the lavender lady fair and square.

My briefcase companion's first words were, "Have you accepted Jesus Christ as your Lord and personal Savior?" I've since learned the only effective answer to that question is, "Screw off." But, caught off guard, I muttered, "Sort of."

Without comment, he opened his enormous Naugahyde satchel and began handing me papers—a large prayer calendar, slick-skinned pamphlets, purple mimeographed tracts, little books, and several bookmarks picturing Jesus.

My new friend asked me to keep his shared treasures in order. I didn't know what that meant, but said, "Of course."

The first was a brochure, "St. Peter and the Roman Cardinals." My guide began his discourse by explaining how all Roman Catholics would burn in hell "forever and ever, amen." During his monologue on Catholics, he was holding and gently stroking a copy of *The Amplified Bible*. He appeared to be inspired by the tactile action and only stopped stroking the study book when I spoke—which was rarely.

He asked my religion. Again, I've since learned the correct response, which is "None," and if you really want to deflect the inquiry, "Democrat."

The truth is that my dog tags showed "Catholic" as my religion, right under my blood type. That way, if my life was threatened, I'd get O positive blood and if my life was ending, I'd be administered Last Rites. Nice package.

My dog tags

Stroking his Bible, my pal was explaining how the first pope really lived in the 5th or 6th century, just as the lady in lavender approached us at a trot. She was holding her pill box hat in front of her with both hands. I strained to see around my rotund, very vocal vicar and his holy briefcase and half stood doing so.

As the lavender lady passed, I could see that she was sick—sick enough to nearly fill her lovely hat with the residue. I thought, "What's with all this barfing?" I thought maybe it was the continuing stench from Don's duffel bag that triggered the incident.

I could see the back of Don's neck from my seat. It had turned a pale green. I turned my attention back to my proselytizing buddy and listened with new interest as he rubbed his holy book and explained how the crusades would have succeeded had Baptists been invited along. I offered a quick thankful prayer for the blessings of Jesus and His wondrous messengers.

Wand

We arrived in Bristol, Tennessee, around sunset. We would be changing railway lines from the Norfolk and Western to the Southern Railway. The conductor told us there would be a three-hour delay in departure. The train offered ham sandwiches (no mayo, no mustard, no cheese—just ham and two pieces of squishy white bread) and warm 7-Up in dirty green bottles. We decided to find a local restaurant, agreeing that railroad towns were famous for having fine blue plate eateries near their stations. The town of 20,000 offered few choices.

We saw a sign, "Wanda's Grill and Fish Shack." Under normal circumstances, we would have looked harder, but we were hungry, tired, and carrying our duffel bags again, since the conductor had suggested we not leave them in the car if we left the train. Wanda's was open.

It was also empty. No customers, no help. We sat in a big booth near the front and waited. Don coughed after five minutes. I went to scout for service after ten. The restrooms were empty. No one was in the kitchen, but the back door was open and emptied into an alley, where I found a woman sitting on a crate, drinking coffee and having a smoke. She was studying the sunset through the transformers and wires of the electrical substation at the other end of the alley. I asked her if she worked at the Fish Shack. She yawned and said, "Yeah. I'll be with you and your buddy in a minute."

I went back to give Don the happy report. Within another 5 or 10 minutes, "Wand" (as her broken name tag read) showed up, looking fully caffeinated and nicotined. I suspect her arrival had more to do with the fading light than a desire to be helpful to two hungry sailors.

I ordered a burger. Don wanted to know what kind of fish was available and whether he could get it broiled. Wand said the fish was "fresh and fried." Don said that would be fine. She brought us Cokes and silverware and left, then came back amazingly quickly with two plates and plopped them down.

Don's fish may have been "fresh" at some point of the manufacturing process, but that was likely months ago. I also have doubts about how it was warmed—I wouldn't say cooked. It was four sticks of stink. It smelled so bad, I couldn't discern any aroma from my grayish burger. Neither Don nor I had any appetite within five seconds of the sticks hitting the table.

We paid Wand our bill, and Don left a tip. We brought my burger with us and shared it once upwind of Wanda's while sitting on our duffel bags. Eating anything inside the Fish Shack was out of the question. The shad stench was smothering. Not one bite of the "fresh fried filet" had been taken. Within a couple of hours, we had regrets about swallowing any of the burger as well.

Lurch

The seats in our new car were more uncomfortable than those in the last one. They were probably more uncomfortable than Wand's crate.

We were on the local. Every few miles, our train slowed and ground to a stop. Sometimes the stop was at a small town's well-lit station, other times, in darkest nowhere. Our train bucked hard twice when it started and labored loudly to a screeching halt when it stopped.

The coach chairs did not recline. There were no footrests. There were hard lumps in the seat. I found the most comfortable position to be with my duffel bag horizontal across my lap. I could bend over and rest my head on the middle and drift off into semi-consciousness.

The lurching starts, however, caused my 60-pound pillow to roll off my lap. I placed the carrying strap under my arms and behind my back, which kept me snug for several stops and starts. I drifted off.

The lurch that ruined my near-nap was in another dark nowhere zone. It was strong enough to send my bag, with me wrapped around it like a strip of raw bacon, headfirst to the floor.

We eventually fell asleep, but the sleep was fitful and restless. I woke up as the conductor announced we had arrived in Chattanooga. As he passed by us, Don asked how long before we got to Nashville. The conductor looked amused and said, "We're not going to Nashville." Don and I were confused. I asked what time we'd get into Memphis. "Late afternoon," he replied as he walked away smiling.

We found out that the trip to Memphis from Bristol was 500 miles—the distance between Boston and Washington, D.C. Our slow train was making minimum progress as it passed through the heart of the Deep South. I was sure we would pass through Tennessee quickly and be on the home stretch.

12-Gauge

Somewhere along the way, we had acquired a dining car. The conductor announced breakfast was being served in the car immediately behind ours. Don and I were first in line. We filled our bellies and went back to our seats. Although our seats were as hard and lumpy as before, we fell right to sleep.

I woke up and noticed we had stopped again. The car was almost empty, and Don was still sleeping. The thought of cold beer and hot soup had a sudden attraction.

I headed for the dining car. Don and I had made friends with the staff, and I couldn't wait to pick up where I left off with the bartender.

As I approached the door, a large red-headed fellow with a shiny 12-gauge shotgun in his arms stood up and blocked my way. He said, "You can't go back thar." Looking intently at his gun, I managed to tell it I wanted some food, please.

12-gauge said, "The next car is closed." I asked it what it was doing on our train, and it announced that it was guarding the prisoners in the next car.

"Prisoners?"

12-gauge explained it was "takin' them boys to Mississippi."

I let it know there had to be a mistake. I was going to Memphis, not Mississippi. It suggested I speak with the conductor, moving with the smallest of jerks toward my right ear. 12-gauge didn't need to speak to communicate. I returned to my seat.

I might have napped after that, but visions of 12-gauge haunted me. Don was impervious.

Continued in Coastin' Part 3 – Un-Tennessee

Coastin' Part 3 – Un-Tennessee

Idlin' Hand

....

Don was asleep. I don't think he was very comfortable. His left hand was perched on top of his head, and he was bracing himself with his left elbow pressed against the window.

I leaned over Don to get a magazine wedged next to him and the bulkhead. He awoke.

He gave me an intense, almost threatening stare as he opened his eyes. "Get it off," were his only words. Caught unaware, I asked, "What did you say?"

"Get it off!" he repeated in a voice pinched with anger.

"Don, get what off?" I asked.

"The water balloon," he barked.

A long pause followed. I had no idea what Don's water balloon could possibly look like. I finally said, "The water balloon?"

"Yes," Don continued, "You put a water balloon on my head while I was asleep. Now get it off!"

I gently said, "Don, there's nothing on your head."

"Oh, yes there is," Don hissed. "I can feel it."
I decided to be silent and study the situation as it played out.

"Jim, I'm going to grab it and if it's a water balloon, I'm going to kill you," Don threatened.

He snatched up his right hand and grabbed his left wrist. He brought the sleeping appendage down to eye level in a quick snap. He looked completely surprised to see his left hand.

We laughed. A lot.

Old Bodies and Spare Parts

Between Corinth, Mississippi, and Memphis, Tennessee, it's junk cars. Every decade back to the 1920s is represented. Some remains have splotches of paint, but most have a burnt rust look. There are great heaps and singletons. Some have their tops cut away. Few have tires. There are no hub caps.

They seem to attract stalking weeds, and most rest in sandy soil unfit for much but wrecks. Several are enclosed by sheet metal fences with gaps and holes. The train is tall enough to look over the fences of these first-line capitalist firms' inventory.

The only thing that outnumbers them is their droppings. Miles of hubcaps kept isolated from their parents, some smooth and others with spokes, in sets and singles. Walls of them lined in neat rows and ranks. "BAIT" is spelled-out on a frame shack in shiny hubcaps.

As we near Memphis, we see the tires—mounds and mountains of tires. The ones on the bottom haven't seen the sun for 20 years. Strangely, there are no whitewalls. I wonder if this represents a racist predilection or if the whitewalls are beyond the means of the local dealers of dead tires.

One of America's greatest graveyards is on that stretch of tracks. The steel and iron bodies slowly molt through the seasons. The caps hang like battle trophies, and the abandoned worn black shoes are stacked high.

It is a melancholy sight—a mix of sad decay and hopeful redemption. They were made to appeal and propel with purpose. As accidents, age, and decline set in, all the classes, styles, and colors became less recognizable as they rusted and lost vitality. They awaited a possible second chance, determined only by their final value as spare parts. From several thousand feet up, they may approach a cryptic kind of art. From a train window, they are endearing.

Hot Winter Night in Memphis

We crept into Memphis at 3 p.m. We couldn't find a cab, so we schlepped our duffel bags toward the buildings downtown.

We walked to the river. We walked through slums. At 5 p.m. on that Saturday night, we found William Len. The hotel had only one vacant room. We took it.

William Len Hotel key

I had my first shower in three days. While Don was taking his, I did some bookkeeping. Our trip had cost me $170 so far, including my share of the hotel room. I had $7 left.

After Don finished his shower, he checked his funds and announced he had $9 and an uncashed Coast Guard paycheck. We decided to cash the check the next day.

The room was toasty. The only window would not open, and the radiator was cooking. It had no valves, knobs, or switches. I was familiar with trying to sleep in heat from my youth in Florida on muggy summer nights before air conditioning. It didn't work for me.

I knew how to engineer cooling off, by dampening the sheets. We tried, with no luck. Don and I had already taken one shower and weren't planning on another. You could walk around outside to get your mind off the heat, but we had seen all of Memphis we wanted. You could listen to music to try and forget the heat, but the room had no radio.

Don went to the tub and began rubbing cold water on his feet. We agreed it was time to complain, so Don called the front desk. No one answered. I got dressed and went to the lobby. No one was there or apparently anywhere on the main floor.

When I got back to the room, I found Don asleep in his bed. The door to the bathroom was open and Don had turned on the shower's cold water and was letting it run.

The door to floor's hallway was open three inches, with the room's only chair blocking the door from closing. The hall was appreciably cooler, and the room was no longer stifling. He was in bed with his duffel bag tied to his wrist. I created a similar nest in my own bed and dropped into a deep sleep.

$4UR

Millington base and the U.S. Naval Aviation Training Center, approximately 20 miles north of Memphis, was our destination. We had to be there by 2400 hours on March 10. Early Sunday morning, we asked at the front desk about transportation to Millington. They suggested a cab. The fare was $20 for both of us, but we didn't have it.

We asked where the bus station was located. "Just around the corner," we were told. The clerk there told us buses didn't run to Millington. We asked where we could cash a government check. He replied, "It's Sunday, good luck."

We could see a sign from the lobby window on a building across the street, "$$4URBLOOD," so we decided we'd each sell a pint. We crossed the street as a fellow was coming out of the blood buyers. He said it was $10 a pint. $4UR was your standard issue life-leaching establishment. We filled out no forms, but we did have our fingers pricked by a gal in jeans before being ushered to two vacant tables. No waiting and step right up.

While being strapped and jabbed, Don asked if I'd ever done this before. Nope. He looked a bit pale as he watched the blood ooze from his right arm and somewhat paler when he saw them stick me. I was fine.

After pulling the hoses out of our arms, they gave us some very sweet orange juice. We were both fine.

The gal in jeans gave us each a $10 bill, and we were better than fine.

I took a header on the curb in the alleyway and woke up looking at a street sign that read, "November 6th Street." I knew pretty quickly that was not the date when I took my nap. I was disoriented and would only learn much later the alley was named for the date the Tennessee Valley Authority began. I took another wee nap.

I awoke sitting in a lounge chair in the William Len Hotel lobby with my locked duffel bag tied to my wrist. While disengaging myself, I heard Don behind me, talking with his mouth full. I was hungry.

I slowly began to stand. Two white sailor caps fell off my head. I almost lost my balance in the confusion. Don came over to me and explained he'd placed the caps on top of my Donald Duck hat so that when I came to, he would see the caps move and he'd come check on me. I thought that was brilliant—in a way thoughtful, and yet somewhat cruel in the way three hats on your head appears to others. My hunger interrupted my thoughts. I had country fried steak.

U.S. Naval Aviation Training Center

We got a cab just outside the lobby. The cabbie agreed the fare was $20. Don confirmed with, "That's $10 each, right?" Yep. We made the front gate in about 40 minutes, and there were no hassles with the cabbie.

We reported to the duty officer at dusk. Our orders were processed, and we were given directions to the barracks. We were even offered a ride, but we opted to walk. We slung our bags on our backs using the back straps like a pack for one last go of it and set out for our new home.

We agreed our adventure was a fine one. It had been expensive and tiring, but a kick. We relived the water balloon-hand part with each of us putting our left hand on our head and then suddenly jerking it down with our right—mugging a look of great surprise as we brought our arm down to our eyes. Lots of laughter on that walk.

As we passed a large construction site, a big cat with a long tail ran out from behind a trailer and stopped in the middle of the sidewalk. Don and I slowed our pace as we neared Tabby so we wouldn't scare her. She didn't move. Six feet away, in the dimming light, we saw Tabby rise up on her hind legs.

"Rat!"

We dropped our bags immediately and ran most of the way back to the guard station. We asked the DO if his offer for a lift still stood. He said yes and arranged for a van. We got back to where we'd left our duffel bags, but before putting them in the van, we approached them cautiously, circled them slowly, and kicked them gingerly. This may have confused our Navy driver.

We were probably the first Coasties he'd seen, and our ways were strange to him. He made no comment.

Later, as we reminisced about our travel exploits, Don and I agreed the rat part was the worst.

("Alice's Restaurant" by Arlo Guthrie was getting play time on local radio stations, and we all found the part about the draft humorous. We were surprised when on March 31, President Lyndon Johnson announced he would not seek re-election. He also ordered a partial bombing halt of North Vietnam and was urging Hanoi to begin peace talks. The news from Vietnam was discouraging.)

Locally

The local news from Memphis had edged its way into national news reports. A strike by black sanitation workers and other Department of Works employees had started in February and gotten uglier by the week.

On April 3, in support of the sanitation workers, at the Mason Temple in Memphis, Rev. Martin Luther King, Jr. delivered his "I've been to the mountaintop speech" in which he foreshadowed his death with the words, "I may not get there with you, but I want you to know tonight that we as a people will get to the Promised Land." On April 4, he was assassinated at the Lorraine Motel in downtown Memphis. Racial unrest erupted in over 100 American cities.

The Navy training base was placed on lockdown immediately following a riot at the noncommissioned officers' club soon after the shooting. All liberty and leaves were canceled.

Coughs and Snores

Although Vietnam was as chaotic as ever, the situation in Memphis and on base had calmed. By early May, Don and I had started going to Memphis on the weekends. There was a movie theater on base, but it didn't feature current movies. Don really wanted to see *The Producers*.

I agreed that would make a fine outing. We caught a ride downtown with some sailors and took a city bus to the theater. Don was recovering from the flu and had a nasty, persistent cough, but he was determined to see *The Producers*. He had a couple of coughing fits on the bus that clearly disturbed some of our fellow passengers.

We spotted a drugstore a few doors down from the theater. Don bought two bottles of cherry cough syrup with codeine for the show. We got to the movie about an hour before it started.

I loaded up on popcorn and Coke, and Don bought several Reese's peanut butter cups. The lights were still on in the theater, and we were the first ones there. We picked seats a few rows back from the front, with me sitting on the aisle and Don next to me.

The crowd started arriving, and Don had another coughing fit. He took a few baby sips from his cough medicine and soon quieted. The theater was filling up rapidly, and soon every seat around us was taken. Only a few seats remained unclaimed in the front couple of rows.

Don began eating his peanut butter cups, which made him cough. He took several more baby sips of his medicine. The trailers were finishing up, and Don's coughing stopped. The movie started, and he passed out. He started snoring. Loudly. His breath reeked of a toxic mixture of cherry and peanut butter.

People started shushing him. I managed to wake him up with some light shaking, but he started coughing again. More people hushed us. Don sipped more cherry cough syrup and passed out again within a few minutes.

He began snoring again. People in our row and the two rows in front of and behind us started getting up and moving down front, realizing Don would either be coughing or snoring. Regardless of their protestations, those were the two options. Or move.

Before the first reel was over, we had no one around us on either side, behind us, or in front of us. Don had established a noisy, stinky island for us in a sea of movie lovers. I enjoyed the show, although I missed large segments of the dialog. Don got some nice rest.

Barracks Life

We had settled in nicely at Millington. We had made friends with several Navy trainees and met them in town on a few of our several trips to Memphis. School was going well. We were moving into studying electronics equipment, and we both enjoyed it.

I was playing cards in the rec room and was winning with regularity. I heard some chatter, followed by a strange sound I was unfamiliar with. Listening more closely, I thought it sounded like moaning.

We stopped the game and joined the few trainees gathered around the TV on that late Wednesday, June 5 night. I heard NBC reporter Charles Quinn say, "He's lying here on the floor. Senator Kennedy has been shot. He's been shot. There's blood on the floor." The TV room was still. Sailors and Marines from throughout the barracks began streaming in. It was tragic.

It felt much like November 1963, maybe worse.

Give Me Memphis, Tennessee

Peggy's

In mid-July, a week before my 21st birthday, Joey and Doug, who bunked in the same area with Don and me, were talking about two women they had met a few days earlier and how they partied all weekend at their apartment. They wanted Don and me to go with them to the party that night at the same place. There would be beer, dancing, and fun.

We stopped at a liquor store on the way into Memphis and bought a couple of bottles of Rebel Yell and a case of Pabst. We finished one bottle of the bourbon before hitting the city limits.

Janette and Carolyn had sublet a two-bedroom apartment from two law school students for the summer. It was on the top floor of a two-story complex near Memphis State University. A guy answered the door and invited us all in. The first thing I noticed was that the doorway to the tiny kitchen had a pop-top chain curtain separating it from the living room. Cool.

Archie Bell and the Drells were singing "Tighten Up" on the phonograph. Cooler, yet. The décor was black and red. The half-dozen partiers were holding beers. A few minutes later, I noticed a shortish girl dancing with a big guy in the middle of the room to "Just a Little Bit" by Roscoe Gordon. I didn't know that song. The girl was cute and soulful with a remarkable smile and laugh. That was Carolyn.

"Nette," her roommate, was a great dancer. When I saw her frolic to The Doors' "Light My Fire," I was impressed. She laughed easily, and, although I was getting a strong buzz, she seemed to like my humor.

The roommates had planned a night of listening to R&B at Peggy's Patio on Mississippi Boulevard in South Memphis—a rhythm and blues music club and grill in a black neighborhood. Don and I were invited to join in. Don drove his used Mercedes, and Carolyn joined us and Joey so she could give directions.

I had continued to drink and was feeling it. Entering South Memphis, I realized I really needed to pee. Really, really needed to. I told Don to pull over. Everyone in the car but Don said, "No." We were in a slummy block in a run-down neighborhood. The front yard of some stranger was not the ideal place to relieve myself, but it had to do. Don pulled over. I got out, swaying a bit, and did my business beside a tree in the dark. Everyone in the car yelled for me to hurry. No one was amused. The car had become quiet.

We made it to Peggy's, and it was crowded. Music was coming from the back of the bar. The place felt right and smelled of French fries boiling in grease. In the back room, a black guy was pounding the hell out of an ironing board that had been converted into an electric piano. He and his drummer were rocking it with the song "Cherry Pie." A couple began dancing on the tiny dance floor.

Ironing Board Sam

We were the only white folks in the place. We were seated at a table near the music, and the beer soon followed. I danced with Nette and then with Carolyn to Ironing Board Sam's (Sammy Moore's) version of "Anyway You Wanta." I sat out to listen. I was wobbly; I was louder than wobbly; I was cruder than loud; but I was mostly sloppy.

A very big bouncer tapped me on the shoulder, picked me up under the armpits, stood me up, grabbed my collar, and marched me out to the front restaurant. He placed me in a booth in the back, next to the juke box, telling me to stay put until he said I could move. I did. He brought me coffee and squishy French fries, which helped. He allowed me to return to our table. No one wanted to dance with me, and I didn't want any more beer. The evening ended with few goodbyes thrown my way. I had blown it. Badly.

Socks

The following week, Don, Joey, Doug, and Fish planned to go back to the apartment for another weekend-long party. I hadn't been invited. Don reassured me with, "You haven't been disinvited." I was reluctant but really wanted to redeem myself, particularly with Carolyn and Nette. I had thought about their dancing and laughter all week. Nette entered my thoughts frequently, but my conversations with Carolyn made her stand out. To try to get back into their good graces, I decided to play the fool—but this time somewhat sober and with intention.

I decided to wear white socks. That simple. White socks with military, spit-polished black shoes made me quite the oaf. I looked ridiculous in my civvies and military footwear. Just what I was after. I got Don to go along with the gag.

My white socks

When we entered the apartment, I wasn't welcomed like the others, but almost immediately Nette and Carolyn spotted my socks. Huge laughter, even a little pointing. I apologized for my behavior the previous week and was pooh-poohed. I asked Carolyn to dance to The Young Rascals' "I've Been Lonely Too Long." She did. That would continue.

Parties

The parties always began on Friday night, with music playing the whole time. I discovered songs like "Michael" by The C.O.D.s and "A Quiet Place" by Garnet Mimms and the Enchanters. We played spades for hours. Dancing and Pabst Blue Ribbon beer were always featured.

The party gang at the apartment

We'd catch a few hours of sleep at some point, finding our way to one of the two bedrooms and crashing on the double bed. The covers were never lowered, and our clothes always stayed on. At times, two or three people might be stretched out on a bed. There was no sleeping schedule. Folks just found their way to dreamland organically.

After a few weekends, we all recognized we were in a special place with our friendships. I was attracted to both Nette and Carolyn, and I flirted with both.

Instant Love

....

It's a Saturday night at the apartment. I've just stretched out on the right side of the bed. Doug is on the other side. "Soul Man" by Sam and Dave is playing in the living room. It is very late, and people have started looking for sleep, although Steve, Nette, and Joey are still up. I remove my shoes (no white socks now) and stretch out. A bedside lamp is on, and its 40-watt bulb is dim. As I begin to drift off, I hear someone come in the room. I open one eye and see through my squint that it's Carolyn.

She goes to the other side of the bed and rolls Doug into the middle. He does not wake. She takes off her shoes. I open my eye a bit wider and see her sit on the edge of the bed, her back toward me. She has a PBR, which she puts to her lips and takes a deep slug. She places the beer down on the night table and turns off the light. I sleep.

At daybreak, I feel the bed shake. Opening one eye again, I see Carolyn stretch, sit up, reach over, and pick up the beer she'd left there the night before. She shakes it twice, then puts it to her mouth and takes a long swig and swishes it in her mouth. She's quiet but thorough. She swallows. I am in love from that very moment. Finishing the same beer she ended the night with as an early morning mouthwash gets me, but not nearly as much as shaking the can twice, to check for cigarette butts that some unthinking fool may have put in the can while she was sleeping. That tells me she has done this before. More than once.

....

The Beach

It was a 12-hour drive from Memphis to Ocean Drive, South Carolina. We got to the beach house early Saturday morning, August 31. There was plenty of room for the seven of us, including Joey's girlfriend who joined the party. We began listening to beach music straight off. I had heard some of the songs before, but many were new to me. I was aware of Jimmy Ruffin's "Gonna Give Her All the Love I

Got," but "I've Got A Sure Thing" by Ollie and the Nightingales was a discovery, as was the shag—the Carolina shag, to be precise. It is a partner dance, and the music is an up-tempo 4/4 beat. Joey and Doug were from Carolina and were accomplished beach music dancers. Joey and his girlfriend were amazing.

At Ocean Drive—Steve, Doug, Joey, Joey's girlfriend, me, Carolyn (Nette photographer)

That night, we drove 15 miles to North Myrtle Beach to find some live music and dance the shag. I wasn't very good at that. Carolyn was almost able to keep up with Doug, but Joey and his girlfriend ruled the room at The Pad, a wooden beach house with a downstairs bar offering cheap beer, washtubs for coolers, and a yard for dancing.

Carolyn and I took a break. As we walked out, we heard "Sixty Minute Man" by The Dominoes. We walked past the pavilion to the pier and about halfway down leaned against the rail. We were talking about the future. She was firm about getting her degree, most likely in English education. I responded with, "After the Coast Guard, I'll get my degree to teach on the G.I. Bill." Without much thought, I continued, "I'm never going to get married. But if I did, it would be to someone like you."

I knew I meant it, but wondered if I should have said it. Carolyn replied, with more grace than I thought possible, "Me too." We kissed with the night breeze sweeping over us. I could hear the waves lap against the pilings. Beach music from The Pad drifted by us. I was thankful and very aware of the moment and of Carolyn—more than I believed possible.

Carolyn and I were now more than just friends. We smiled at each other with the knowledge.

Steve, Carolyn, and Jim at Ocean Drive

Fall

Upon our return to Memphis, I completed the last few weeks of school at Millington. Carolyn and Nette had to move when the fall semester started at Memphis State.

Carolyn moved in with Maggie, a close friend of her family. I visited her on the weekend, and she cooked dinner for Maggie, Nette, and me—a first. It was good.

Maggie and Nette disappeared, and Carolyn and I took advantage of our privacy in a way not yet shared. It was grand and then some. Our pledges of love were permanent, as it turned out, and not just declared in a moment of passion.

We played some records and danced. Clarence Carter's "Slip Away" sang us out.

I received my orders to report to the U.S. Coast Guard Aviation Center in Mobile, Alabama, on September 30. Mobile was as close to Memphis and Carolyn as I could hope. I left Memphis on September 22 to tears and promises and returned to Plant City to visit my folks. I spent a good portion of the day and evening on the phone with Carolyn. My mother asked me with a knowing smile, "Why didn't you stay in Memphis with Carolyn?" Excellent question.

Carolyn on the phone with me in September 1968

Stuck Inside of Mobile

Airfield

Mobile had its allure. It's a mid-sized port city on the Gulf of Mexico, 40 minutes north of the narrow beach of Dauphin Island and an hour from the party beaches in Biloxi, Mississippi. The clear water and white powder sand of Destin, Florida, is 100 miles east. New Orleans and all its treasures is a three-hour drive west. Memphis is a six-hour drive north. Carolyn too.

Mobile had its stench. It was home to two paper mills. In an unfavorable wind, the fumes from Scott and International Paper made eyes water and throats choke. Forty miles southwest, Pascagoula, Mississippi had a fishmeal plant that equaled paper manufacturing in olfactory assault. It was impossible to ignore the smell of Mobile. Let's call it the Mobile Mist.

I reported to the Coast Guard Aviation Training Center at Bates Field, about ten miles west of Mobile, and lived in the barracks area of the hanger. I was learning to fly. Although still wingless, I was taking my first flights on helicopters and amphibious airplanes. As a flight crewman, I was sometimes the navigator, sometimes the radioman, always the observer. I enjoyed the time in the air, except when the invisible Mobile Mist blew in.

When I wasn't in the air, I was an aviation electronics (avionics) bench technician. I was not good at troubleshooting. I was very good, however, as a radioman for the base and ended up being assigned that role frequently. I worked several search-and-rescue missions, successfully coordinating with the in-air crews and those supporting the missions on the ground. I relished the overnight shifts as a radioman and was recognized for my performance—all in all, a decent start as an air-sea rescue man and avionics technician.

Navigating the Distance

Carolyn and I were writing almost daily and calling each other several times a week for hours at a time. The calls were rapidly adding up to more than the cost of a plane ticket, so I bought a ticket. I was to leave on October 18 and fly back two days later.

We decided our relationship was serious enough for me to meet her parents. Her mother and dad, Christine and Clyde, met us at Carolyn's brother's house in West Memphis. Bill and his wife, Sue, made us feel welcome. I loved Clyde immediately. He was a man's man, yet kind and full of good cheer.

Christine was a mostly serious lady with strong religious views. I knew I needed to work on Christine. I was very familiar with strong-willed Christian southern women and knew how to avoid alienating them. Using all the charm in my reserve, I got her to laugh a couple of times. She didn't hate me. Clyde liked me.

Back in Mobile, I decided to get away from barracks living. I got the necessary paperwork processed to move off base and qualified for a $60 monthly housing allowance. I found a roommate in David, and we rented an apartment at Dauphine Apartments in mid-city Mobile. Lots of Coasties rented there, so friendly neighbors were assured. I also found it easy to carpool with fellow Coasties back and forth to the base.

Dauphine Apartments, Dauphinwood Drive, Mobile

Carolyn arranged a quick trip to Mobile for November 8, and I scrambled to move in a couple of days before. The apartment was furnished, but the gas and electricity had not been hooked up.

David planned to visit his parents the weekend Carolyn was arriving, so we had the apartment to ourselves. It was cold. Thirty-six shivering degrees cold. We ate little but peanut butter and jelly sandwiches and went nowhere. We were broke, cold, and hungry. We were deeply in love and mostly stayed in bed. We snuggled and caressed, even though Carolyn slept in her coat. It was divine.

Carolyn returned to Memphis, and I went back to flying, soldering new components into black boxes, and working the air station's radio systems. The cost of our phone calls was breaking us, even though we wrote frequently. We decided rather than sink more money into AT&T; we would meet in Plant City after the Christmas holidays. We knew it was time for me to introduce her to my family and friends. She feared meeting Gene and was even more intimidated by my sister Judy and asked me not to leave her alone with either.

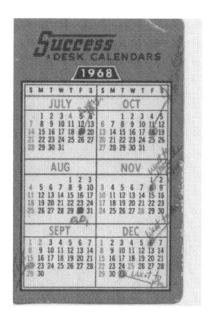

Carolyn's 1968 pocket calendar

Bringing Her Home

Carolyn and I flew to Tampa from Memphis and Mobile, respectively. We arrived in Plant City on New Year's Day. Judy and her husband, Charlie, had been visiting my folks over the Christmas holidays and were scheduled to leave late that afternoon to return to their teaching jobs in Miami.

We were all determined to make Carolyn feel comfortable with us. Everyone got along fine. Judy was very pleasant, and Charlie was charming, telling outrageously funny stories and doing a world-class impression of the French skunk cartoon character, Pepe Le Pew. My mother liked Carolyn from the get-go, and I could see Carolyn warming to her. Pop, too, thought Carolyn was good for me. He did slip up early on, referring to Carolyn as "a Georgia girl." Carolyn quickly corrected him with, "No, that was the last one." Pop got a kick out of her quick retort.

I introduced Carolyn to my grandparents Foster. They took to her immediately. She would be spending nights with them while in Plant City, and we would connect after she had a leisurely breakfast with the Fosters each morning. Each day, their relationship deepened. I slept in my old, very small bedroom at the back of my house. I had no desire to sneak out the window. I would never sleep in that room again.

For lunch New Year's Day, Pop cooked his renowned porterhouse steaks. They were two inches thick, aged, and cooked to order. He was skeptical of Carolyn's being able to finish one of these monsters, but she did herself proud. That little test of eating big at the Helms table was all she needed to win the family over (that and how well we complemented each other). I informed my family at the end of the meal that we intended to get married the following July. Everyone was delighted with the news. Judy and Charlie left immediately following our feast. Carolyn had held her own with Judy.

January 2 was Carolyn's birthday, and Pop, Keeta, Carolyn, and I were going out for dinner. She needed a dress, so I took her to see my grandmother, Zula, at her Helms Dress Shop early Thursday morning. Carolyn knew how close I was to Mom Helms and was looking forward to meeting her.

Mom Helms picked out a dressy frock for Carolyn in the most current style. She looked great. I complimented her extensively—against my natural disdain of commenting on women's choices in dress. By the time we made the purchase, Carolyn was completely enamored of Zula. Zula also clearly approved of her.

In a private moment, Carolyn and I discussed our plans for her return to Mobile with me on Sunday so we could be together a few more days. I had lied to my parents in telling them that she would be going to Memphis but we instead bought her a ticket to Mobile. We decided to sneak away from Plant City. Just as my parents left the airport concourse and disappeared from sight, Carolyn ran up with her carry-on and joined me before the cabin door closed on the flight to Mobile.

(In Vietnam news, 1968 would close with 549,500 U.S. troops in Vietnam and 16,592 U.S. service personnel killed, and 87,399 wounded at that point in the war.)

Revved Engagement

As much as we looked forward to spending time together in Mobile, we were distressed about separating at the end of the week. Carolyn was working at Union Planters Bank, and her vacation time had almost expired. We couldn't afford for her to lose her job, but maintaining our relationship from 350 miles away would likely drive us into real poverty.

Neither of us wanted to be apart any longer. After a couple of hours of discussion, we realized we were waiting to marry for the sake of our families and friends. We also knew we didn't want to wait and couldn't afford to. That was it. We decided to get married immediately.

It would be a huge challenge to obtain licenses and blood tests, arrange for a marriage officiant, find a location, and identify witnesses. We went to work.

We called our families, beginning with Carolyn's parents. We were worried about everyone's reaction, but since my sister and Carolyn's sister had also eloped and been forgiven, we thought we might have the same good outcome. Christine and Clyde were completely taken off guard, but after longs pauses and a lot of questions, they finally came around and wished us well. However, they said that getting to Mobile by Sunday was not possible. Clyde offered to bankroll Carolyn's wedding dress.

We next called my parents, who were even more shocked than Carolyn's. My mother had little to say. Pop expressed some reservations. I reminded him of Judy and Charlie's spur-of-the-moment marriage. He replied that they had known each other for years. They gave us their blessing finally, but they, too, said they couldn't make the trip to Mobile on such short notice.

We called our siblings. They offered varying degrees of support. I called Mom Helms. She was pleased but declined our invitation to attend.

We finished our family calls with Mom and Pampa Foster. Their immediate reaction was, "That's wonderful!

Congratulations! We will be there tomorrow. Don't do anything until we get there." I had no doubt spending time with Carolyn a week earlier had convinced them that I knew what I was doing. I asked Roy to be my best man, and he agreed instantly, saying he was deeply touched. They asked if my parents were going to the wedding. We told them they had wished us well but would not be attending.

Mom and Pampa Foster arrived the next afternoon. Before they checked into their motel, they took us to get our blood tests, apply for a marriage license, and visit Trinity Episcopal Church on Dauphin Street in mid-city Mobile. They waited in the car for almost two hours while we met with Father Ben McGinnis.

At first, Father McGinnis tried to convince us not to rush into marriage. We asked if we could marry us on January 12, the upcoming Sunday. He said that would be impossible. It was Super Bowl Sunday, and he already had a wedding scheduled after the game. After much more talk, we convinced him to marry us after the 10:30 a.m. worship service. That worked for us, and Father McGinnis could still see Joe Namath and the New York Jets.

We began calling friends. Gene was skeptical. Carolyn's roommate Nette was delighted. She said she would find a way to get to Mobile to serve as Carolyn's bridesmaid. Carolyn and I retired that night in total bliss.

Foster Support

On Friday, Zola bought Carolyn a negligee. Carolyn broke out Clyde's checkbook and wrote a check for a lovely white wedding dress and coat. At the same time, Roy was buying me a spiffy suit, so I wouldn't have to get married in my Coast Guard gear. Everything was coming together.

We then went to Sears and bought a new TV. Zola said we must have one. We had decided to skip the ring exchange in the ceremony, but Roy would have none of it. He told us to go to Goldstein Jewelers and pick out some rings. He told us if we were still married in five years, we could pay him back. We thanked him, but instead broke out Clyde's checkbook again and bought our modest gold bands. Mine cost $16, and my bride's was $9. It was the last check Carolyn would write on her parents' account.

Saturday at midday, Clyde and Christine surprised us by showing up, and soon after, my folks arrived. Carolyn and I were overwhelmed. My parents had brought a negligee with them that my other grandmother Zula insisted they give to Carolyn. At dinner with our families at Wintzell's Oyster House, I convinced Pop and Roy to take me out to a strip club along the Mobile waterfront.

It was a hardscrabble bar, but we were there so early it was just us, the barmaid, and a lone, friendly stripper. She entertained us well, removing Pop's glasses and giving them a body-excursion in her bosom. All three of us laughed uproariously. Roy slapped Pop's back, but modestly declined having the stripper take his own glasses on a similar journey. It was the first time I'd ever seen Roy and Pop enjoy being in each other's company.

Me and my best man

Be Wed

Our wedding party the next day was 12 people strong, including the priest and the bride and groom. Earlier, we had received a call from New Orleans. Carolyn's bridesmaids Nette and Sue-Day, along with three other friends who were not in the wedding, had stopped in New Orleans the day before, partied late, and overslept.

Nette begged us to delay the wedding a few hours, until they could make the drive over. I was pissed, Carolyn crushed. We explained it was impossible according to Father McGinnis. We scrambled to find a bridesmaid. We called John, a fellow Coastie, and his wife, Bonnie, agreed to serve.

Our families, John and Bonnie, and my roommate David found their way to the small chapel in the church. We sat in the waiting area just outside the chapel. In a quiet moment, my mother sought out Carolyn and confided in her with, "I am going to give you the only advice I'll ever give you. Don't live in the same town with me. I have lived in the same city with my parents and in-laws, and my husband and father didn't speak for 30 years. That wounded me deeply. It almost ruined my life." Carolyn knew about the dysfunction in my family and, holding Keeta's hand, thanked her and promised to take that advice.

Father McGinnis appeared, and the ceremony began. It went off splendidly. During the exchange of rings, I closed the deal by reverting to my three-year old Elmer Fudd voice: "With this wing, I be wed."

Carolyn and Jim leaving the church after their vows

Acknowledgements

Several people provided essential assistance and support in writing the stories, and I wish to acknowledge them. Carolyn Helms, my wife of 50 years, was my primary audience and critic throughout the research and writing and rewriting of the stories.

Anne "Chickie" Barresi was my editor for the work and provided invaluable corrections and suggestions on writing style, proper punctuation, and word usage. Her application of strenuous professional language standards to the work not only led to proper word usage but improved readability. Her ability to inject outrageous humor in her ongoing editorial comments throughout the review process made the writing even more enjoyable.

Patsy Ambrose Sjostrom was extremely helpful in translating key phrases in the book from the spoken word to the written. Rodney McGalliard and Carl Lane offered advice early on that was beneficial in the layout of the work. Gil Gott of Plant City Photo Archive was helpful with my research for much of the work.

Numerous others read galleys of the stories, providing critical feedback and offering helpful contributions to the content of the work. These generous people include my Uncle Bobby Helms, Janette Richards, Rich Curd, Chuck Bennett, Joey Aiken, Don Christian, Niki Cassidey, Claude Earl Lynch, and Doug Harbin. Others providing supplemental content included my classmates from high school—Ken Keller, Selinda Walden, Julie Holbrook, Dub McGinnes, Sherry Kelley Sims, Ann Bender, Bobby Pyle, Tommy and Diane Brown, Peg Laseter Lee, Sylvia

Robbinson, Trina May Brown, Cinthya Miley, Diane Cook Sparkman, Virginia Brosbt Tharrington, Peggy Gibbs, and Charlie and Lianne White.

Another set of folks offered much needed encouragement throughout my writing, took the time to read my galleys, and offered me reassuring feedback. This group includes my sister-in-law Shirley Brackin and her son Chuck, my brother-in-law Bill Chism, my cousin Alma Foster, Bob Bedgood, Sue Conger Caughman, Pete Waller, Ali Barresi, Kris Sjostrom, Meghan and Ben Lane-Danz, Rosemary Lane, Sally Peterken, Dr. Gary Nelson, Kevin McWhorter, Chris Dittes, Jim and Micki Gager, Barbara Hartman, Barbara Wintzer, Todd Thomas, Heidi Marggraf, Jeff Wunderlich, Dr. Mark Genco, Cindy Crean, Laurie McCarthy, Shelby Bender,and particularly Dave Wells.

Me signing the word "sister" in front of Zula's fence

Available from :
Lulu.com
with desktop

Amazon.com
with mobile device

Made in the USA
Columbia, SC
06 July 2020